LIVING A
LIFE OF
JOY

LIVING A LIFE OF JOY

JOHN
RANDOLPH
PRICE

FAWCETT COLUMBINE · NEW YORK

A Fawcett Columbine Book
Published by Ballantine Books

http://www.randomhouse.com

LIBRARY OF CONGRESS CATALOGING-IN-PUBLICATION DATA
Price, John Randolph.
    Living a life of joy / John Randolph Price. — 1st Ballantine
Books ed.
        p.   cm.
    Includes bibliographical references.
    ISBN 0-449-91138-1 (trade pbk.)
    1. Spiritual life.   2. Joy.   I. Title.
BL624.P754   1997
299'.93—dc21   97-21724
                                                                CIP

Text design by Holly Johnson

Cover design by Kristine V. Mills-Noble
Cover photo © Chase Swift/Westlight

Manufactured in the United States of America

First Edition: October 1997

10 9 8 7 6 5 4 3 2 1

To Ralph Waldo Emerson, who encouraged us to "work a revolution" in our lives with greater self-reliance and a new respect for our inherent divinity.

CONTENTS

CONTENTS

INTRODUCTION

Despite appearances to the contrary, a tidal wave of change is turning the world around—and our lives with it—sweeping away the old order and taking us from a negative doctrine of sin and suffering to a positive spirituality of goodness and joy. It is a revolution that began six centuries ago, and the pace has quickened to where it is now moving with great velocity to show us the true meaning and purpose of life.

After the long night of the Middle Ages—the millennium of the medieval church—came the Renaissance. It was a new era of freedom of thought and a spirit of rebirth, with men and women *changing their minds* about themselves and their world. This led to the Age of Enlightenment in the eighteenth century—a period of new self-confidence, freedom, and optimism. Next came Romanticism (late 1700s to the mid-1800s) when people focused on the way they would like things to be rather than as they appeared. Great emphasis was placed on the individual and the virtue of simplicity. It was also the time of the "new mysticism" and the birth of Transcendentalism, which was based on the doctrine of self-reliance.

As this revolution in mind and heart advances toward climax in our time, we see all that was good in these movements coming together in a crescendo of positive change—and we hear the fervent call for personal discovery, illumination, and a bold new interpretation of life. There is a renewed emphasis on freedom and optimism, the beauty of simplicity, and the courage of self-reliance. There is even a broad and passionate revival of "mysticism," defined in Webster's *New World Dictionary* as "the doctrine that it is possible to achieve communion with God through contemplation and love without the medium of human reason."

The men and women throughout the world who are following this inner path are the visionaries and intuiters of today—the new Transcendentalists—and perhaps the words of Emerson are echoing in their collective thoughts. He said that we "shall introduce a pure religion."[1] "The foregoing generations beheld

God and nature face to face; we, through their eyes. Why should not we also enjoy an original relation to the universe? Why should not we have a poetry and philosophy of insight and not of tradition, and a religion by revelation to us, and not the history of theirs."[2]

It has been my good fortune to know many of these shining lights and their "philosophy of insight and not of tradition, a religion by revelation." Through their understanding and practice of joyous living—and by their fruits—they are leading us into the new world, and along the way they are breaking through the superstitions and myths that have held humankind in the bondage of guilt for so long.

They have provided a road map, handed down through the ages, to a higher realm in mind and heart where all things good, true, and beautiful eternally exist. It is a guide to a higher coordinate in consciousness where we are free to love unconditionally and to live life for the pure joy of it. It is a plan to complete the revolution from darkness to light.

The map consists of specific directions to that City not built with hands—an atlas of parallels and meridians, of deserts and mountains, byways and overpasses, falls and rapids, and safe habitats for moments of rest. To help explain certain aspects of the journey I've included a few personal stories to show where I experienced wonderful demonstrations of the law of harmony on the high roads and toll-free express lanes.

Yes, I have taken the trip, and although I haven't reached the ultimate destination yet, I have learned a few things about reading the road signs that may be helpful to you.

The trip begins with a look at our point of departure—where we are now in terms of attitudes and beliefs. The roots of good and evil are then exposed to show where humanity's progress and problems originated. This understanding and heightened discernment will be important during our travels. We will also meet the invisible society of people who convey messages to inspire us and instill courage along the way, and then study the detailed instructions on how to travel the principal highways and avoid the dead-end roads and unsafe interchanges.

On the trip we will enter the dancing atomic structure of physical form, move into the etheric ring—the mold of the fleshly vehicle—to balance our energy centers, cross the troubled waters of the astral plane and see where our emotions are making waves, and on into the mental realm where we will begin to *think* and use our minds constructively. From there our journey will take us into the clear light of our spiritual nature where we will discover that whatever it is we seek is already a part of our reality. To fully experience this sacred environment we will learn to live with love, forgiveness, and wisdom. We'll look at the effectiveness of prayer and the activity of Divine Influence, move into a deeper awareness of the nature of God, and carefully work with the principles of what it means to "live the good life" from the higher vision.

As our understanding grows we'll notice that the outer scenes are appearing more beautiful day by day, our physical system will seem to be operating on a higher energy level, our finances will be more abundant, and our relationships will move into greater harmony. And we'll hear ourselves laughing more, not taking things so seriously as we truly enjoy life—perhaps as never before.

Come. Take the journey with me. We'll travel light.

PART I

PREPARING
FOR THE
JOURNEY

1

POINT OF DEPARTURE

As part of our travel plans we should know where we're coming *from*, where we are at the present moment. To do this we need to establish a benchmark, a reference point in measuring our attitudes and beliefs, and make an honest appraisal of our spiritual understanding. In essence, we want to look at how much unnecessary baggage we've been carrying around and get rid of everything except the essentials. Remember, we want to travel light.

First, how much truth do we know? And what is truth? The ancients said it was thoughts in conformity to reality. *Whose* reality? It's easy to see how the subject of "truth" can turn into philosophical white water, so let's go back to what we believe—and to do that we only have to look at our lives. We are what we believe. If we are experiencing illness, limitation, and friction, we are believing in lies that have become our truths. A victim consciousness descends, unworthiness produces failure, guilt calls for punishment, and fear attracts that which is feared.

There was a lunch counter on the first floor of the office building where I worked back in the '70s. While I was grabbing a quick bite one day a man came in and sat on the stool beside me. He ordered the blue plate special and said, "Worst food in town," then proceeded with an angry tirade about the crime wave that was engulfing the city and "the thieving and murdering animals" that were lurking in every shadow. It was obvious the man lived in fear, and his parting words were, "Guess I'm going to have to get myself a gun." I've often wondered what happened to him.

If we were watching and listening from the other side of the veil to determine the predominate "truth" registered in the collective consciousness, we would conclude that it is indeed a state of fear. How can fear be represented as truth? Convictions of perceived reality constitute the lowest level of what the human considers his or her truth, and to most people fear is a fundamental fact of life. Therefore, what is feared is believed, it becomes a person's truth, and this fear-truth can be expressed in one of two ways:

as an inhibited life of withdrawal from the world to escape the object of fear, or as aggression to mask the fear and satisfy a need at any cost. In both cases there is an inability to trust God and the natural process of life, but it is the people in the second category who are triggering a dangerous reaction in the mind-aggregate.

The unified mental-emotional depository is now weighted heavily in favor of the idea that objectives must be achieved regardless of the consequences to others, that the end always justifies the means—with actions corresponding to that mind-set. For some this is translated into reaching goals as a tunnel-visioned workaholic; for others it means "anything goes" in the greed-pursuit, and people who get in the way are nothing more than pawns in a master game of desire fulfillment. The darker the mind with fear the more unreasonable the deed, which often results in fanaticism in the name of God, Country, and any cause to which the individual is paying allegiance. And fanaticism leads to terrorism—acts of force to threaten, intimidate, and cause injury and death, based on a belief.

What a person believes becomes that person's truth, with or without any moral or ethical foundation. We see this in the subjugation of women in the family unit—the countless reports of abuse, marital rape, and other tyrannical behavior. We see it in racial conflicts and in the treatment of minorities, in the underhanded scheming and manipulation in the work-place to achieve one's ends, in the shabby machina-tions on every level of government, and in religious intolerance throughout the world.

So what do we do? We begin by changing our own thoughts and perceptions, and focus on what *we* believe as our way of preparing for the journey to the higher altitudes.

HOW CLOSE IS OUR TRUTH TO *THE* TRUTH?

And what is *the* truth? *The* truth represents the eternal verities from our Creator that have been known by the masters of wisdom since the beginning of time. For example . . .

> *God is the infinite absolute All Good Creator,*
> *the sum-total of all energies, forever one with*
> *Its creations, loving fully and expressing com-*
> *pletely in every good and perfect way.*

My religious background began in the Baptist church, Sunday school mostly. Then one Sunday when I was nine or ten I went into the church with the big people and heard the preacher talk about a punishing God. I thought the man was insane and never went back to that church. I found other places of worship that placed the emphasis on a loving God, which I intuitively knew was the truth.

When a violent, judging, punishing God is talked about in the Bible, particularly the Old Testament, the reference is not to the Supreme Deity but to a god created in the image of man and projected into the world as an arrogant, angry, jealous ruler. Contrary to Jesus's teachings, the early Church accepted this view of God. Clement, Bishop of Rome (circa A.D. 90–100), wrote that "God, the God of Israel, alone rules all things: he is the lord and master whom all must obey; he is the judge who lays down the law, punishing rebels and rewarding the obedient."[1]

God, Clement continues, "delegates his 'authority of reign' to 'rulers and leaders on earth.' " Who are these designated rulers? Clement answers that they are bishops, priests, and deacons. Whoever refuses to "bow the neck" and obey the church leaders is guilty of insubordination against the divine master himself. Carried away with his argument, Clement warns that whoever disobeys the divinely ordained authorities "receives the death penalty."[2] His God was obviously created in the image of man and remains as part of the collective consciousness.

It is difficult to understand why the belief in a false god continues when for thousands of years the true God has been revealed by the saints, sages, mystics, and masters in every culture, race, and religion. There is only an infinitely loving God whose Mind could not conceive of anything so humanly created as a pit of fire for lost souls. There are no lost souls because we are a part of God and God cannot be lost. This is a benevolent universe with consciousness as the key to life on every plane of existence. God does not give, take away, reward, or punish. *God is love indwelling, forever expressing all that is good, true, and beautiful in life—nurturing, nourishing, caring—never judging, angry, or vindictive.* Such a God could not exist except in our minds, so let's remove from consciousness any false and limiting ideas concerning our Father-Mother Creator.

> The truth about yourself:
> *Each person is God in expression as individual being.*

Whether we have realized it or not, we are immortal spiritual beings temporarily clothed in a physical body. God-as-all-persons is a truth honored by every culture of antiquity. "Voltaire said that Plato should have been canonized by the Christian Church, for, being the first propounder of the *Christos* mystery (the indwelling Christ or true Self of everyone), he contributed more to its fundamental doctrines than any other single individual."[3] A few hundred years later Paul affirmed Plato's understanding when he wrote about "the mystery which has been hid from ages and from generations . . . Christ in you, the hope of glory" (Col. 1:26–27). And "Christ liveth in me" (Gal. 2:20).

In the Nag Hammadi texts, discovered in Egypt in 1945 and considered older than New Testament gospels, we are told that "whoever perceives divine reality becomes what he sees."[4] We have seen the divine reality because every soul was anointed in the beginning as a direct expression of God. Therefore, in our heart of hearts we intuitively hear the inner voice speak to us of the truth of our divine Self:

> *The will of God for you is done, carried forward eternally on wings of love, expressing as your Self, the anointed one.*
> *You are the Light, the first immortal One; no other exists except the illusion in mind, the lie who leads in fear.*
> *Know yourself as a Shining One, eternal being of heaven and earth, the One who leads in wisdom and understanding.*
> *Master the unholy self who creates discord and blinds the vision of truth, and peace and wholeness are yours.*
> *Forgive yourself for the fallen creature you thought you were, and have mercy in your condemnations, for you have risen.*
> *Be Thyself, now and forever more.*

These words are speaking to each one of us—to all humanity—to plant the seeds of remembered divinity, for it is the understanding of who we are that sets us free.

Every being is eternal, every soul is universal, every person is divine. Only one *I* has ever lived, and that is the Holy Self of God. This is the truth, regardless of the individual, the place, or the circumstance. It simply *is*—with no possibility of refutation or denial, except from the ego.

The truth about life:
Life and spirit are one, unified as all and present at every point. Life is infinite unfolding joy with deep meaning and true purpose.

Our life is God-Life, eternal, abundant, and perfect. It is a Divine River, without beginning or end, ever-flowing from the one Source to quicken and vitalize us. Life *is*. It cannot be destroyed, created, or changed into something else. "Life is the energy in expression of the divine will-to-good."[5] Are we fully accepting that expression?

Let's think about those aspects that seem less than ideal. Do we believe that certain relationships are responsible for a less fulfilling life? Or is it a scarcity of money? Our health? The political arena and government in general? Let's remove from our consciousness any and all ideas that we can be limited by someone or something in the phenomenal world. Since our life is the expression of the divine will-to-good, disharmony cannot prevail unless we accept it. So let's set aside and forget for a time all concerns we have about the physical-material effects we see in our lives. And somewhere along the way as we travel to the mount we'll discover the truth that there was nothing to be concerned about. The problems were not real; they were only thought-forms projected out of mind.

> The truth about death:
> *There is no death, only a continuation of eternal life.*

Life cannot die; consciousness cannot be extinguished. We simply take our awareness and understanding of our identity with us when we are freed of the physical body. We then find ourselves living fully on another plane of existence, and we realize that death was only an illusion of the mortal mind.

I remember telling a couple of my friends that our minds live after death—that there isn't such a thing as death, we just move from inside the house to out-of-doors. I was six years old at the time, and my friends ran home after hearing my pronouncement. It frightened them.

As my wife, Jan, wrote in her book, *The Other Side of Death*, "There is no such thing as death, the end of life, or the 'final curtain.' Death is nothing more than a transition, which means passage, transformation."[6] Her visit beyond the veil during a near-death experience gave her a firsthand opportunity to prove the continuity of life and the great joys that await us when we have completed our mission on the physical plane.

What we're seeking on our journey is a new state of consciousness—a literal heaven on earth—but if the fear of death is packed away in the luggage of mind, it's going to make a heavy load. So let's leave it behind. Let's not worry about when or how we'll make our transition. That's up to the higher nature, our Soul, which determines our time of departure. In the meantime, let's concentrate on *living* fully, joyfully experiencing each moment in physical life.

The truth about time:
*Time does not exist on the inner planes and
    can be altered to conform with conscious-
    ness on the outer.*

We can rise above the limitations of time when we understand that spiritual consciousness transcends all concepts of the human mind. However, when we are operating strictly within the confines of ego, time becomes the scapegoat: "I don't have enough time." "Where does time go?" "If I only had more time." Poor time. It gets blamed for so much. No wonder it hides when we need it most.

The truth is, time only has power in the physical world that we give it. Doreen Virtue, Ph.D., and author of *I'd Change My Life If I Had More Time*, has written: "When we believe it takes a long time to get a new career, a different house, or a better relationship, it *does* take a long time. But when we believe it's possible for changes to instantly occur, then they do! The bottom line is this: *Whatever you believe about time—that you have plenty, or that you don't have enough—you are correct!* There are no limits to the changes you can make in your life, and there are no time shortages except those that are self-imposed."[7]

Jan and I have worked with the idea of condensing or changing time, and it's amazing how time becomes amenable to consciousness. Let's keep that in mind while on our journey, frequently reminding ourselves that time obeys us, and not the other way around.

The truth about infinite possibilities:
This is a loving universe where every good and perfect possibility exists.

Nothing is impossible, and that includes the understanding that there is no reality in illness, scarcity, failure, or discord. With this uplifted consciousness we see that we are spiritual beings living in a spiritual universe where the fullness of a "life more abundant" is the absolute principle of being. That is when the Essential Self takes over, and while the manifestation appears as a healed body, financial abundance, creative success, and loving relationships, it was our Spirit simply revealing the harmony that had been there all the time.

To understand this proven principle we need only to keep our minds open and receptive to that which is considered strange, unknown, mystical, and miraculous. And as we do, we'll see the proof that all things are indeed possible.

Can we accept the idea that we are multidimensional beings operating simultaneously on various frequencies of consciousness? Could we agree that we should be able to travel through space-time parallels to other worlds? Can we accept the possibility that healings from all manner of disease and mortal wounds can be done spontaneously? Can we open our minds to the likelihood of instantaneous manifestation of visible form out of energy? And would it not be to our advantage to understand the reality of the twenty-two archetypes who live in our auric field as aspects of our divine Self so that we may have true dominion over "this world"?

Nothing is impossible. Let's make that our mantra as we travel to the summit.

Now, if God-as-Love is all there is, life is the divine will-to-good and there is no death, time is our servant and nothing is impossible, then why do we have problems? Just where did evil originate? In preparation for our journey let's probe the mystery of polar opposites for the answers.

2

THE ROOTS OF GOOD AND EVIL

When Jan and I were on our West Coast book tour in April of 1996, several people at the book signings asked about her pronouncement that no one has ever done anything wrong. This was a teaching from beyond the veil and reported in her book. One man in Santa Barbara became quite disturbed and asked about the "evil" people who walk the earth. When she referred to *consciousness* as the key to all actions—saying that regardless of what we've done, all is forgiven—he became even more confused.

The fact of the matter is that no one is either a sinner or a saint—we only act out of the consciousness where we are at the time—and the punishment or reward is nothing more than the impersonal and educative law of cause and effect in action.

Let's understand that the essential Self has never thought, felt, or acted wrongly. This indwelling Reality doesn't even know the meaning of the word sin. It is the human *personality* with its false beliefs and emotional baggage that expresses both harmfulness and harmlessness depending on the frequency of mind and heart at any given time. Yet even the Hitlers of this world are forgiven because God loves unconditionally and knows the actions were nothing more than consciousness in expression. They could not have done anything differently—thus no punishment is decreed by a higher power. Yes, such individuals will go through *self*-punishment until a balancing of the heart-mind energies eventually takes place and they are restored once more to normalcy. This may be a difficult concept to accept without an understanding of both the law of cause and effect and the principle of unconditional love.

So do we say that there is no such thing as good and evil? We say there are no polar opposites in reality—everything just *is*, eternally being in a state of perfection. In the sleep state, however, which most humans and visible nature are experiencing at this moment, we do have two sides of the coin, and in the world of duality we must be judicious. "All is God," a wise one once said, "but I would not stick my head in the mouth of a tiger. He may not know he is God, and a bite would be quite natural and not considered wrong to the animal." Think about this and its application to the *human* kingdom.

Yes, there are people in this world who would be considered amoral—neither moral nor immoral. Our judgment here is to know that they do not have the capacity to distinguish between right and wrong; that's simply their consciousness. But we're not fearful of anyone because when we're living in the higher frequencies we are essentially invisible to those working out of the lower energies. That doesn't mean we need not be discerning. Until we awaken from the illusionary dream we have to be cognizant that people are playing certain parts on the stage of life that appear to be villainous. And while we know that the energy of forgiveness is constantly pouring through them from above, and that the law of cause and effect will eventually bring forth a resolution, it still behooves us to understand where they're coming from. This will help us to live with less anger, fear, and resentment—a necessity if we're going to reach the Land of Peace and Plenty.

Consider now all the *personalities* that have expressed on Planet Earth since the beginning of third-dimensional time—from the lowest to the highest and all the shades in between. What I am pointing to here is that the collective consciousness is the sum-total of all the personalities of all the people who have ever lived. Some were honorable and altruistic; some were unprincipled and heinous; most were in the broad middle ground with varying degrees of good and evil in expression at any given time.

Now we bring in the principle of *like attracts like*—which means that an individual's energy will draw that person to a similar group energy. This is what happened over millions of years on what is known as the astral plane, finally resulting in the emergence of two planetary Archetypes long before the time of recorded history. Consider the idea that for aeons following the creation of the phenomenal universe, individualized spiritual beings took on physical form in order to experience dense matter. They became trapped in a material existence and lost (although not forever) their consciousness of dominion.

Fear was the the first negative emotion registered, which bred all manner of other characteristics of denial such as anger, hate, jealousy, resentment, and condemnation. There were also those who remained separated from a consciousness of materiality and who maintained a conscious awareness of their true identities, thus radiating the energy of love, harmlessness, selfless sharing, harmony, and peace.

The mind energy of these combinations of souls

and all who were to follow was/is deposited in the collective consciousness, giving it life, intelligence, and power. The dominant strain in each category emerged as the focal point of supremacy—a Leader Mind representing the whole of the parts—a concentrated Energy Field within the collective consciousness functioning as an Archetype, which is defined by Webster as "a perfect example of a type or group." And so two Archetypes became manifest in the race mind, appropriately called *The Dweller on the Threshold* and *The Angel of the Presence.*

John Jocelyn, a spiritual teacher and philosopher, wrote that "The Dweller on the Threshold is the result of all unredeemed evil, and today we see mankind as a whole facing its Dweller. This is an astral entity; it feeds upon the foul food of the lower regions of the desire or soul world with its murderous desires . . . we must face this demon and dissolve its evil force. This dissolution would not be possible save for the sum of all our good forces. . . ."[1] Referring to the Greater Archetype (the Angel of the Presence), Jocelyn says, "The power given to us by this beautiful, benign being, the embodiment of all our good and truthful thoughts, feelings, and acts as well as all that we may yet become, allows us to face the fiendish Dweller on the Threshold and to dissolve it wholly."[2] Between the Dweller and the Angel we have the perfect example of duality and poles of opposites.

These immense energy fields are radiating centers of force that reach and influence essentially everyone on the planet, each according to his or her dominant vibration in consciousness. People functioning primarily in their lower natures will naturally attract the rays of the Dweller, while those in higher states of consciousness will be more in tune with the Angel. This receptivity to one or the other led to the formation of two distinct forces on the physical plane, appearing at the dawn of what we now consider ancient civilization. Those with the lowest vibrations—called the "Dark Forces" in Ageless Wisdom—became consciously aware of the Dweller Archetype and appointed themselves "priests" in its name, attracting others of like minds to maintain the world in bondage. Those were the initial souls who were trapped in dense physical matter and who identified only with their bodies and their selfish miscreations in the world of form. Separated in consciousness from their spiritual nature, they saw only conflict, competition, destruction, and death—because that was the world they were projecting on the screen of third-dimensional life.

The actual formation of a secret society under the influence of the Dweller began as a protective measure, i.e., by joining forces with their enemies and possible assailants they would have a greater sense of personal security while building a stronger group power base. The number of people who physically became identified with what we will call the *Brotherhood of the Shadows* is not as important as the multitudes who joined its ranks and participated on an *unconscious* level. A nefarious mind-link was established throughout the world, essentially of one accord with the Dweller Archetype. By tracing the events of history from ancient times to the present we can see the primary objectives of this group: Divide and conquer and create disunity whenever possible by organizing opposing forces, maintain conflict as the natural order of humanity. Why? Because the Dweller was created out of such energy and can maintain its own life force (consciousness) only by continuing to draw on this misqualified energy.

Conversely, the Angel Archetype—representing the inherent truth and beauty of the human family—has its own frequency, and those in tune with it bonded together (also on an unconscious level) as a Force for Good. This was the beginning of the *Society of Light* and a collective return to the original Divine Estate. Its objective: spiritual understanding, love, unity, and world harmony. We get a clear view of these opposing forces in this passage from *Esoteric Psychology, Volume II*:

> As you know, on the astral and mental planes, centres exist which are called 'dark centres', because . . . all energy is subordinated

for purely selfish purposes. As I have stated before, the Forces of Light work with the soul, hidden in every form. They are concerned with group purposes, and with the founding of the Kingdom of God on earth. The dark forces work with the form side of expression, and with the founding of a centre of control which will be theirs entirely, and which will subdue all the living forms in all the kingdoms, to their peculiar behests. It is the old story, familiar in Biblical phraseology, of the kingdoms of the world and the Kingdom of Christ, of the power of the anti-Christ, and the power of Christ. This produced a great climax in Atlantean days, and though the Hierarchy of Light triumphed, it was only by the merest margin. The battle was fought out on the astral plane, though it had its correspondence upon the physical plane, in a great world conflict, of which the ancient legend tells us. It ended in the catastrophe of the Flood. The seeds of hate and separation have been fostered ever since that time. . . .[3]

To assist me in my own understanding I prepared a list (obviously incomplete) showing what I considered the influences of the two Archetypes. You are encouraged to add your own ideas to the lists.

INFLUENCES OF THE COLLECTIVE CONSCIOUSNESS ON HUMANITY

The Brotherhood of Shadows: Activist-attack groups that cannot tolerate beliefs contrary to their own, apartheid, censorship, drugs and drug cartels, economic depressions, end-of-the-world religionists, erosion of individual rights, ethnic unrest and divisions, feudalism, the Holocaust, imperialism, the Inquisition, isolationism, racism, religious extremism, slavery, terrorism, totalitarianism in any form, and wars.

The Society of Light: Ageless Wisdom, the Bill of Rights, the Constitution, Declaration of Independence, democracy, environmental action, equality, free enterprise, free speech, global cooperation, justice (true), humanitarianism, individual rights, international spirit of goodwill, the New Thought movement, the peace movement, positive future, spiritual fellowship, spiritual freedom, unconditional love, and world unity.

Djwhal Khul, the Tibetan master who provided the materials for the Alice A. Bailey books, has written that, "A gigantic thought-form hovers over the entire human family, built by men everywhere during the ages, energized by the insane desires and evil inclinations of all that is worst in man's nature, and kept alive by the promptings of his lower desires. This thought-form has to be broken up and dissipated by man himself."[4]

How do we do this? Understand that each one of us represents the Dweller Archetype when we live in the lower nature of our personality. Therefore, as we lift our consciousness we are literally denying the Dweller its sustenance. But what about the other people in the world who are not concerned with humanitarian issues and who are not aware that they play a part in the planetary chaos through their thoughts, feelings, and actions? Let's not forget that the Angel Archetype is silently and powerfully radiating all that is collectively good and true into individual minds. And while these people may not be receptive on a conscious level, the energy is being registered on some deeper plane of consciousness.

Also, as we reduce the projections of the Dweller by lifting our own energy vibration, the indifferent and unaware people within the range of our consciousness will be positively affected. And we must remember that there are millions of men and women on earth at this moment who are living in a higher state of spiritual understanding—and from the standpoint of spiritual physics, right is always mightier than wrong and good is more powerful than evil.

Practically speaking, it all goes back to what we can do individually to lift our consciousness into the higher frequencies and join in the work of the new Transcendentalists. I believe it would also be helpful to understand more about the man who brought us those "new tidings" in the 1800s, Ralph Waldo Emerson.

Why Emerson and not some religious figure from the sacred texts? For one thing, he gave us "The Declaration of Independence for American thought"—and his principles are part of a Golden Cord of Truth that was first anchored in Ageless Wisdom, pulled smoothly through the writings of all religions, and woven into the fabric of our consciousness. Emerson is real to us, and perhaps because he wasn't a saint we can more easily relate to him. It is reported that the elder Henry James was horrified when he saw Emerson smoking and enjoying a glass of wine, as though one with a spiritual consciousness would not do such things.

Emerson was indeed genuine, and the order of thought from this truly American hero can be the connecting link to the Universal Mysteries that have been ours since the beginning, waiting for us to hear and know once more. "The criers of the Mysteries speak again," writes the eminent philosopher Manly Hall, "bidding all men welcome to the House of Light. The great institution of materiality has failed. The false civilization built by man has turned, and like the monster of Frankenstein, is destroying its creator. Religion wanders aimlessly in the maze of theological speculation. Science batters itself impotently against the barriers of the unknown. Only transcendental philosophy knows the path. Only the illumined reason can carry the understanding part of man upward to the light."[5]

Because of Emerson's integrity and forthrightness, his stature as the Sage of Concord, and his standing as one of America's greatest writers, he can be accepted by all of us as a major prophet of spiritual idealism. Therefore, Emerson can well be called the point man to show us the proper direction for our journey.

Let's learn from him and then begin our inner travels with a twofold purpose: to dissolve our individual connection to the Dweller, and reach the secret place of the Angel of the Presence.

It is time.

3

THE NEW
TRANSCENDENTALISTS

Theodore Parker, a prominent Christian minister, social reformer, and a Transcendentalist of the nineteenth century, stated that the purpose of Transcendentalism was "to revise the experience of mankind and try its teachings by the nature of mankind; to test ethics by conscience, science by reason; to try the creeds of the churches, the constitutions of the states, by the constitution of the universe."[1]

Parker was describing Emerson's idea of seeking the true nature of things, using intuition as the method of distinguishing between appearance and reality. The roots of this philosophy can be traced back to 1833 when Emerson discovered God within himself and wrote about finding one's own salvation through the transcendental method. In *Ralph Waldo Emerson: Essays and Journals*, Lewis Mumford writes: "Emerson was the bringer of new tidings, a modern gospel; but he himself would have been the first to point out that this gospel had always been in existence, since it was wrought into the very nature of man. For Emerson saw that man's mind was the focal point for the forces of the universe, and that experience was incomplete until it translated the dumb language of natural objects and events into the conscious language of the mind, while that language itself required further translation into action: (quoting Emerson) 'A thought which does not go to embody or externalize itself is no thought.' "[2]

Emerson wrote, "We live in succession, in division, in parts, in particles. Meantime within man is the soul of the whole; the wise silence; the universal beauty, to which every part and particle is equally related; the eternal ONE. And this deep power in which we exist and whose beatitude is all accessible to us, is not only self-sufficing and perfect in every hour, but the act of seeing and the thing seen, the seer and the spectacle, the subject and the object, are one. All goes to show that the soul in man is not an organ, but animates and exercises all the organs; is not a function, like the power of memory, of calculation, of comparison, but uses these as hands and feet; is not a faculty, but a light. . . . From within or from behind, a light shines through us. . . ."[3]

Emerson believed that a direct relationship between mind and Spirit could be achieved through intuition, thus transcending other forms of communications—not only from the senses but also what was being preached from the pulpits and taught from the Scriptures. He knew that the ultimate truth could only be found through the cultivation of a spiritual consciousness and being receptive to the word of God spoken from within.

The new Transcendentalists are now in every area of society—government and politics, education, economics, entertainment, the arts, science, the judicial system, health care, religion, corporate America, and in the small businesses that represent the freedom of creative expression in the United States and abroad. They are carrying the torch of Wisdom from the past, silently stirring our conscience to shake loose from the constraints of present-day life, and helping us to develop a passionate commitment for the future. As Emerson said, we must accept our "transcendent destiny . . . not pinched in a corner, not cowards fleeing before a revolution, but redeemers and benefactors, obeying the Almighty effort and advancing on Chaos and the Dark."[4]

He also wrote, "Let us stun and astonish the intruding rabble of men and books and institutions by a simple declaration of the divine fact. Bid them take the shoes from off their feet, for God is here within."[5] And "It is easy to see that a greater self-reliance—a new respect for the divinity in man—must work a revolution in all the offices and relations of men; in their religion; in their education; in their pursuits; their modes of living; their association, in their property; in their speculative views."[6]

A SUMMARY OF EMERSON'S PHILOSOPHY

There was no question in Emerson's mind of the reality of God, which he called the Over-Soul. He knew that he was born of Omnipresent Spirit and remained forever Spirit in expression as Self, with the Highest and Fullest of Absolute Being dwelling within him. He found his home in God and could sit in that Presence in perfect humility, listening to the inner voice and letting God shine through him.

To obey the inner voice was of extreme importance because divine guidance was always flowing through mind, which eliminated painful decisions and uncertain actions. To hear and follow the Word places us in the right place at the right time and in the right work. He said, "Place yourself in the middle of the stream of power and wisdom which animates all whom it floats, and you are without effort impelled to truth, to right and a perfect contentment."[7]

He also equated the attribute of will with the presence of God, and felt that each individual was continually impressing his or her will on the universal energy, which in turn responded to the individual's character. Thus, we always have "dominion" and our world simply reflects that which we are.

To Emerson, prayer was the art and science of looking at life through the highest vision and pronouncing all things good. Prayer was not to "effect a private end" but to establish oneness with God in consciousness and then see the miraculous activity of God at work. He admonished us to be detached from the effects of this world, to see everything as thought in expression, and to move in mind to the level of cause to release the creative force for the good of all. He said, "Self-reliance, the height and perfection of man, is reliance on God."[8]

Emerson's emphasis on the individual was not a glorification of the ego. In fact, he believed that most people were a bit deranged because they were operating out of the lower nature, yet he knew the truth of everyone—that within every man, woman, and child was the all of Nature, the whole of Reason, the perfection of God. With our Divine Soul we could know all and dare to be all that we could be from the highest perspective.

He believed that all Truth was omnipresent, and as we evolve spiritually we will arrive at that moment when we become consciously aware of spiritual facts, knowing of course that those principles are not new but old and eternal—only our recognizing them is new. But once these eternal Truths are appropriated by mind, we are no longer controlled by fate. We pass into a *higher council-chamber* and a life of sovereignty. And so he tells us to look for our own light of truth, and once we find it and make it our own, to never be dissuaded from it. We let it grow into the great searchlight of the soul, becoming the reality of our being.

Emerson's basic law of life was the Law of Compensation. This is the ancient law of karma, a natural force to enable an individual, a group, and a nation to reap what is sown. Every mental, emotional, and physical action triggers a chain of causation, a ripple effect that moves toward infinity, with each ripple sending back a reaction and continuing until the effect of the cause is resolved. This force is part of the natural order of things and is to be respected but not feared; we must simply learn to work with it. He said, "Cause and effect, means and end, seed and fruit, cannot be severed; for the effect already blooms in the cause, the end pre-exists in the means, the fruit in the seed."[9]

He also had much to say about religion in general and Christianity in particular. Religion, to Emerson, was simply one's relationship to God, the inmost core of being. He felt that historical Christianity had "fallen into the error that corrupts all attempts to communicate religion."[10] It was to be a doctrine of the soul and a revelation of the Christ, and not exclusively a portrait of the person of Jesus. He wrote: "That which shows God in me, fortifies me. That which shows God out of me, makes me a wart and a wen. There is no longer a necessary reason for my being."[11] "The belief in Christianity that now prevails is the Unbelief of man. They will have Christ for a Lord and not for a Brother. Christ preaches the greatness of man, but we hear only the greatness of Christ."[12]

In Emerson's view the Bible was not finished, and that it must not be closed until the last great man is born. He encouraged us all to write Bibles and to "unite again the heavens and the earthly world" by honoring the truth we know and use in our daily lives.

The essence of the Emerson philosophy that influenced me was the idea that there are no limitations except the ones that we place upon ourselves through the failure to know the Essential Self within—and that our vision to be and do is always in line with that which we see through our state of consciousness. If we are in the valley we will see the valley. If we are on the mountain we will see the mountain and the victory of High Cause. We have a choice, and we begin our ascension by deciding first not to be dependent on anyone or anything in the external world for our happiness. All is within—in the God of our Individual Being.

I also love the man for his fire and passion, his

reformist temper, and his disregard for tradition—all made less extreme by his marvelous sense of humor. He cared little for popularity, choosing to risk all if necessary as a spiritual activist focused on changing minds through words and actions. He was foursquare against slavery and was a part of the underground railroad that hid and protected runaway slaves. He was always true to himself and to his mission, which was to create an invisible society of those who would live in the spirit.

With gratitude to Emerson—American essayist, poet, philosopher, and lecturer—for his driving force for change which continues to this day, we move on to see if his ideal of a sacred network was fulfilled, and if so, how we can use it to our benefit in our travels to the mountain.

THE INVISIBLE SOCIETY

In *The Morning of the Magicians*, Louis Pauwels suggests that the awakened ones have indeed formed such an alliance. He writes, "No human being lives alone. He can only develop himself within a society. The human society we know has shown only too well its hostility towards an objective intelligence or free imagination . . . [so] there is every reason to believe that they are working and communicating with one another in a society superimposed on our own, which no doubt extends all over the world. That they communicate by means of superior psychic powers, such as telepathy, seems to us a childish hypothesis. Nearer to reality, and consequently more fantastic, is the hypothesis that they are using normal human methods of communications to convey messages and information. . . . The general theory of information and semantics proves fairly conclusively that it is possible to draw up texts which have a double, triple or quadruple meaning."[13]

Yes, the invisible society does exist. In every city and country in the world there are people who have moved past the halfway point in the awakening process and have become aware of their powers. They are invisible because you seldom hear about them—particularly those in government, education, religion, science, and the higher echelons of the corporate world, in addition to those in what we would consider ordinary jobs leading "normal" lives. They work silently behind the scenes of mainstream life doing their part in making the necessary adjustments in the collective consciousness. Only a small percentage have elected to call attention to themselves, and they have done so primarily in their work of serving others—but even then their "spirituality" is not worn on their sleeves as a badge of honor. And not a single awakened one would ever give the impression that he or she has an exclusive franchise on Truth.

Concerning the idea of communicating messages through transmissions with several meanings, this is already being done in books, motion pictures, television shows, stage plays, and song lyrics. To entertain the mass audience while chipping away at closed minds is one objective of course. The other is to give inspiration and encouragement to those on the inner journey in language that is clearly understandable. You have seen mass-appeal movies with an underlying esoteric theme, and have read "secular" books with different levels of spiritual interpretation. The Light Bearers are busy, and will continue to spread their influence as the collective heart is opened to receive.

I bring up the existence of the invisible society to create a greater understanding that we are a part of a worldwide movement that is bonded on the inner planes and expressed on the outer to create a definite shift in the race mind. And they are with us on the journey to the light, offering advice and counsel through various means as we move through the maze to higher ground. The inspiring messages are everywhere, but we must listen and be alert.

Many years ago the "sustenance" I was given for the trip was a reminder about *joy*. The message went something like this: "Begin the odyssey with joy. Do not wait to find joy at the end of the path. Find it at the beginning and take it with you, otherwise the quest will be arduous. With joy as the beacon the puzzle will be quickly solved and ecstasy will meet you when you arrive."

Shall we begin with joy?

4

BEGINNING
THE JOURNEY
WITH JOY

In *The Angels Within Us* I reported on another instruction I received about joyful living, this time in a dream: "Do everything in life just for the fun of it. Nothing else really matters."[1]

The idea of "fun" in this context may sound strange to many people. It is usually thought of as joy and gaiety from playfulness and pleasure, and may be too frivolous and hedonistic a word for some when applied to spirituality. For others, joy and fun would be acceptable only when conditions of satisfaction are met—certainly not something to focus on as a primary goal in life or as the starting point for a spiritual journey. After all, aren't we here to suffer our way through life so that we can enjoy the fruits at another time in another dimension called "heaven"?

I don't think so. It's my belief that we're supposed to kick up our heels and laugh and play and not worry a whit about tomorrow. And that conviction comes from a deep pool of merriment on some coordinate in my energy field that frequently reminds me of the earlier instruction to find joy *now*—to not wait until later. Also brought to mind is the call for joy in the world's great philosophies and sacred teachings. From the beginning of time as we know it, the affirmation has been for joyous living and the bringing of joy to others—to live life to the fullest—not just a momentary feeling of happiness but living it for a lifetime. Look at the vast number of references to joy and happiness in the Bible, the Bhagavad Gita, and the philosophical writings spanning Plato and Emerson and beyond.

The Bible, with more than ninety references to joy, tells us: *Let the hills sing for joy* (Psalms 98:8), . . . *everlasting joy shall be upon their heads* (Isaiah 35:10), *You shall have joy and gladness* (Luke 1:14), . . . *that my joy may be in you, and that your joy may be full* (John 15:11).

The Bhagavad Gita, the jewel of India's spiritual wisdom, reminds us that the full nature of God is joy and we are the enjoyers. *When one understands the Personality of Godhead, the reservoir of pleasure, Krsna, he actually becomes transcendentally blissful.*[2]

The Great Books of the Western World tell us that Plato "identifies happiness with spiritual well-being— a harmony in the soul, an inner peace which results from the proper order of all the soul's parts."[3]

And according to Emerson, "The way of life is wonderful; it is by abandonment."[4] "Life . . . is for well-mixed people who can enjoy what they find without question. . . . To fill the hour, that is happiness; to fill the hour and leave no crevice for a repentance or an approval."[5]

Tryon Edwards, famed American theologian in the 1800s, wrote, "Happiness is like manna; it is to be gathered in grains, and enjoyed every day. It will not keep; it cannot be accumulated; nor have we got to go out of ourselves or into remote places to gather it, since it has rained down from Heaven, at our very doors."

The Tibetan Master Djwhal Khul asks us to "Ponder on joy, happiness, gaiety and bliss; these release the channels of the inner life. . . ."[6] And in his various Meditations on Joy we read: "The Joy of the Soul irradiates my life, and lightens all the burdens which those I meet may carry."[7] "Let the song of the soul be sounded forth by me, and the clear high notes bring peace and joy to others. My word today is *Joy*."[8]

When Jan visited the other side during her near-death experience, she returned with a deeper understanding of this, having been told quite specifically by her very Soul: *"The purpose of life is joy, and with spiritual understanding the physical senses are enhanced. Savor fully the loveliness of each experience. Self-awareness is the prayer of the heart, and to pray without ceasing is to play. Play with the joyful abandon of the child, absorbed in the delight of each moment. Let go of obligation and duty, and live for the pure joy of being."*[9]

An article titled "Who Is Great?" in *Parade* magazine echoed this appreciation. "In a 1985 study at Brandeis University conducted by Teresa Amabile, now a professor of business administration at Harvard University, a group of professional writers—none famous—was asked to write a short poem. Each writer was then randomly placed in one of three groups: One group was asked to keep in mind the idea of writing for money; another was told to think about writing just for pleasure; and a third group was given no instruction at all.

"The poems then were submitted anonymously to a panel of professional writers for evaluation. The poetry written by people who thought about writing for money ranked lowest. Those who thought about writing just for pleasure did the best. 'Motivation that comes from enjoying the work makes a significant difference,' Amabile said."[10]

Working strictly for pleasure or living for the pure

joy of being is easier said than done you may think, and I would agree—until we break free of the Dweller part of the collective consciousness. How do we do that? The religious texts say the way is hard and those who find it are few. Yet if we turn to willpower metaphysics we find that all we have to do is lift up our consciousness. Ah, we have found the solution. The only problem is, we get so caught up in the hoisting process that we forget how to live—and what life is all about.

So what's the answer? To me it's a simple change of attitude, best described in this way:

There's no sense worrying about anything, everything's just fine.

That's not ostrich or Pollyanna thinking—it's a strategic debilitating strike aimed right at the heart of the ego who loves woe and has elevated the word *victim* to celebrity status. This shift in thinking and feeling will put us into alignment with our true nature where all is perfect right *now*. We don't say it's *going to be okay*. That's pointing to the future, denying the reality inherent in the present moment and indicating that matter and minds have to be manipulated in order for the situation to change. When a seeming miracle occurs to reflect our different attitude, what really happens is that the truth of what already *is* is revealed. We were only seeing an illusion—a projection of an old mind-set—that was obstructing the good which had been there all the time.

I like what Benjamin Franklin said: "Do not anticipate trouble, or worry about what may never happen. Keep in the sunlight." And a couple of thousand years earlier, the Great Example told us to not be anxious about our lives because anxiety wasn't a power to accomplish anything.

What happens to us when we stop fretting and, regardless of appearances, turn our minds to the positive side of life? We loosen up, get lighter, the ego is weakened, and the power from within that reveals the *all good* begins to flow. We may even take time to play a little and let the responsibility for the "serious" part of our lives be handled by a higher wisdom and intelligence. That's when miracles seem to be multiplied daily.

To play, to have fun, to be joyous doesn't come naturally to us after we put on long pants or take the bows out of our hair—in other words, when we "grow up." That's usually the time our self-image kicks in and we begin to see ourselves as lacking, less than, vulnerable—and in our striving to compensate, be more, and protect ourselves we become grim reapers of our own creations.

Whatever we believe about ourselves is reflected back to us in our career, finances, relationships, health, and all other aspects of life. If it's a false belief, the effects will be a direct projection of that belief. As time goes on we hear about "self-esteem" as the answer to all of our problems—and we begin formulating an idea of how we want to see ourselves and how we want others to see us. And sometimes this can lead to an "identity crisis." Let me give you a personal example.

I was continually ill at ease with the career I had embarked on in 1981, having jumped from the very earthy and materialistic advertising agency business into spiritual communications—and the adjustment process took longer than it should have. Even in my first book, *The Superbeings*, I questioned my qualifications "to tell others how to reach the high road to freedom."[11] So it was only natural that I drew that kind of energy to me.

At a workshop in California in the early '80s a woman asked me to list my qualifications for teaching ideas of truth. "Are you a minister?" she asked. I said no. "Are you a psychologist?" I said no. "Are you a counselor?" I shook my head. "Then what are you?" I think my response was that I was just a writer sharing my experiences in life.

Later I thought a great deal about the woman's questions and even more feelings of inadequacy set in, and for a time I seemed to wander in the wilderness trying to "find myself"—to determine who and what I was in my new activity of life. I looked at what I *wanted* to be—a researcher and an author of books based on my understanding of the purpose and meaning of life—but without the "qualifications," I thought, I could never have real credibility. See how easy it is to deny ourselves? That's ego in action.

Then I began receiving mail addressed to The Rev. Doctor Price, and instead of being pumped up I really came unglued. I did not want to be associated with anything *religious*—spiritual is fine but not *religious* because I'm not the pious type and certainly do not adhere to any particular dogma. This disavowal soon attracted someone to say, "Oh, you write religious books." And I responded, "No I do not!" I gave much thought to this attitude of denial and what I finally realized was that I did not want to be considered some sort of mountaintop mystic or a group's guru. All I wanted to do was write for the joy of it without being classified as even a "teacher."

There's no sense worrying about anything, everything's just fine.

The breakthrough finally came on one particular weekend when the gentle voice from within said to get back into consciousness for the healing work. I did, and over a forty-eight-hour period of emotional soul-searching I was taken back to that "era of heart" where I have the deepest feelings—the age of Romanticism in the 1800s. I looked at the philosophical writings of Hugo, Whitman, Wordsworth, Goethe, Coleridge, Thoreau, and Emerson—the emphasis on imagination, on *feelings*, and the supernatural—and their rebellion against established rules and regulations. Who were they? They were *writers from the heart* using their minds to convey ideas and make a revolution, and their only qualifications were their thoughts.

I felt comfortable with the energy of this group and realized that I could live anywhere without credentials, write all types of books for the pure pleasure of it, contribute in my own way to this world, and just be me. I could call myself a writer, visionary, philosopher, but even that wasn't necessary now. My Self-identity had returned, not as a persona or mask to be worn for the benefit of others, but as a greater understanding of who I am in truth—a spiritual being in physical form visiting Planet Earth for a time to share ideas on the healing of consciousness.

Perhaps there is something in this story that will help you quickly move past an identity crisis.

Without true Self-identity we'll find that living for the fun of it is nothing more than an impossible dream. And the nose goes back to the grindstone, the heavy backpack of responsibilities is shouldered once again, and the trudge through the quicksand of life continues. Hopeless futility? Inevitable hardships? Only if that's what we choose—and we do have a choice.

To turn our lives around takes only a moment of decision, a commitment, and the process of transformation has begun. Begin right now. We'll let the child come out to play without worrying about images or impressions, and we'll let the "esteem" part of self apply only to that highest aspect of our being. We're going to stop being concerned about how others see us—*I am who I am*—and we're not going to try to change to meet anyone else's expectations. For once, we're going to be true to ourselves.

If you are not keeping a journal to daily record your thoughts, aspirations, and new spiritual understanding, I suggest you begin now. Write the date and title the entry *My Day of Decision*, and in your own words write your determination to break through all barriers and soar out into the totally unlimited aspects of life and living. This affirmative meditation will help you with your resolve:

> *This is the day, the moment, that I turn away from sadness and sorrow, from lack and limitation, from conflict and chaos. I know this is a benevolent universe and that I was created to live in gladness, abundance, and harmony.*
>
> *So I make my choice now to live lovingly, joyfully, and peacefully—to smile and laugh and sing as I embrace the fullness of life—doing everything for the incredible joy and fun of it.*
>
> *I toss worry behind me, wave anxiety out of the way, and tell fear it no longer has a place to live in my consciousness. I am willing*

to be happy for the rest of my life, and I now
follow the path of ecstasy and bliss.

And along the way we'll be joining with that
immortal part of us in singing the song of joy—for
ourselves, and for everyone we meet as we fly toward
the sun.

PART II

CROSSING THE AURIC FIELD

5

Moving
from Form
to Energy

Plato told us that what we could see and touch was not a reliable measure of reality—that anything "physical" was not a principle or law. By that he meant that what appeared as physical didn't have any power except the power we give it—what we project onto it.

I thought about the time a Doberman watchdog slipped through a neighbor's gate and came galloping down our country lane in my direction, fangs bared.

There's no sense worrying about anything, everything's just fine.

Something in me said (very quickly), "You used to scare the children playing monster—play the game!"

So I played Frankenstein's monster and staggered toward the dog with arms raised, my voice a horrible moan. The dog stopped in his tracks and cocked his head at me. I could tell in an instant what he was thinking: "What in the world is *that*?" He didn't stick around to find out. He turned and sprinted all the way home, sailed over his fence and out of sight. It worked—I had taken away his power to intimidate or harm me. (I'm not suggesting you try this unless you are assured of proper guidance and protection.)

In the Platonic doctrine of reality we find that what we see as "solid" in the objective world—including our physical body and the money we spend—is an image in our mind appearing as solid. Therefore, the objective world has its existence only in consciousness, both individual and collective.

Where does the image come from? It isn't reflected in our minds by God, for God's work was completed "in the beginning." The image is drawn from energy patterns of reality—archetypal lines of force representing the all-that-is of original creation. And the quality of the image is based on the frequency of consciousness with which we are operating, i.e., low equals false, higher equals nearer to real.

How is structure made? By the creative power radiating from Self and materializing as configurations of energy. Take the body for example. What we see at first is flesh, but as we rise in consciousness we begin to see a lighter and finer body, still appearing as physical but more in line with the perfection of the pattern. Rising higher in consciousness we see the light/energy shining in and around and through, and moving even higher we perceive the radiant energy field representing the true structure and absolute perfection of the body. This is the original archetype of "body"—a divine idea forever in perfect expression.

Everything gives an appearance because our minds arrest the energy vibration so that we may perceive the form—and that includes food, clothing, transportation, money, homes—or whatever else we can see, feel, smell, or taste. It is all energy manifesting as a form of energy, which our minds "hold" as matter. Yet the matter is not in itself solid; it only appears that way because our consciousness is interpreting it as substantial as part of our objective world.

Quantum physics agrees. In the book *Quantum Reality* author Nick Herbert writes about reality being "observer created." He quotes quantum theorist Dr. John Archibald Wheeler as saying: "No elementary phenomenon is a real phenomenon until it is an observed phenomenon."[1] Herbert says that Dr. Wheeler's experiment in quantum reality "seems to show that the past is not fixed but alters according to present decisions."[2] "Until conscious observers came upon the scene, the universe existed in an indefinite state. . . ."[3]

He goes on to say that, "The first person to suggest that quantum theory implies that reality is created by human consciousness ... was the eminent mathematician John von Neumann (who said), 'the world is not objectively real but depends on the mind of the observer.' "[4] According to this quantum reality, says Herbert, "dynamic attributes, when not being observed, exist as a wavewise superposition of possibilities; the universe acquires definite values for these attributes only during a conscious observation."[5]

This means that we create our own individual worlds through our understanding of Truth and our personal interpretation of the twenty-two archetypal patterns within, which I call "angels" in my book *The Angels Within Us*. (Quantum physics tells us that the electromagnetic spectrum has twenty-two orders. Coincidence?) Thus we very well do create our own realities.

TAKING A CLOSER LOOK AT OUR AURIC FIELD

If we could step back and view ourselves, the first point of reference would be our fleshly vehicle—a dancing atomic structure that appears to be solid. Around this body of form is a sheath of energy called the etheric body—and the etheric is surrounded by another energy force known as the astral or emotional body. The mental body, the field of the conscious mind, is the next circle of energy—and encompassing, overshadowing this entire energy field is the Cosmic or Light Body, the Divine Consciousness of our essential Self that is seeking a clear path of expression from Cause to effect.

Our Divine Consciousness is Principle. The Principle is this: *I, Principle, HAVE to, MUST, express as wholeness, abundance, and harmony. I have no choice in the matter because Principle is Law and Law is Truth and Truth MUST be expressed. It is the Divine Imperative.*

When we are consciously aware of the Divine Self as Principle, we are in alignment with the Law. And remember that the Self chooses the channels for the expression of good. The channels are the twenty-two Living Energies within, and the quantity of the quality—the measure of the manifestation—will be in accordance with our understanding and acceptance. Whatever we seek—health, wealth, right relations, job, etc.—must be found within consciousness because consciousness is all there is. (For a detailed review of the Living Energies, or the causal powers within that I call angels, please refer to the Appendix.)

Our objective now is to travel in mind through our auric field to this realm of pure Spirit where Will-Power, Love-Wisdom, and Intelligence-Inspiration work in unison as Super-consciousness. We begin with what we can see with the physical eyes.

———

The primary form we identify with as a person is our physical body. This association with materiality is one of the basic reasons for slow progress on the path, and in some cases can even be a major roadblock. Thus, a greater understanding of the visible aspect of our being is necessary at this stage of our journey.

An ancient teaching tells us that when we identify with the form we become vulnerable to decay, for that which appears as solid must in time return to its natural state. The world of form is illusion because it is temporary; the eternal Reality is within. When we focus our attention on what seems to be a malady of the body we are literally releasing *concerned energy* to the affected area and increasing the potency of the problem. *Hold mind to the Inner One and not the discomfort, and the healing energy will flow down, and the impure energy will be withdrawn up from the point of sickness.*

One night while visiting a friend (before my Self-identity realization), I fell off a high deck on to the rocks below.

There's no sense worrying about anything, everything's just fine. Remember, that is *always* true even though appearances may tell a different story. It is true on the inner and will be revealed in the outer as we raise our consciousness.

I was taken to a hospital emergency room and X rays showed a fractured pelvis and hip and severely torn ligaments. I stayed overnight, and this being my first incarceration in such a facility, I immediately began planning my escape.

My first course of action was to send healing light to the broken bones, which was interrupted by the inner voice saying, "Heal your mind and emotions." The healing energy was then directed throughout my auric field, and in a few minutes I found a blip. It was an old error pattern that spoke of my seeming lack of progress in this lifetime, together with a thought-form of self-condemnation. The fall was my subconscious desire to punish myself for this belief, and I felt the guidance from within was saying that by healing my mind I would not only transmute the energy that precipitated the fall, but would also cause a rapid knitting of the bones. I worked on the correction for most of the night, and the next morning I told the doctor I was leaving.

He smiled and said, "Only when you can go up and down the stairs using crutches."

I'd never been on crutches in my life, but I said, "Go get them." When I demonstrated my agility in using the devices on the stairs I was discharged. At home I continued the consciousness-healing process, and three weeks later at a New Year's Eve party Jan and I danced. Later, X rays could find no evidence that the fractures ever occurred.

"Concentration upon the physical body only serves to enhance its potency and to feed its appetites and bring to the surface of consciousness that which should be securely secluded below the threshold of consciousness. The true aspirant should be occupied with emotional, not physical, control and with the effort to focus himself upon the mental plane, prior to achieving a stabilized contact with the soul."[6]

"When the physical body becomes, in error, the object of attention, retrogression is indicated; and this is why all profound attention to the physical disciplines . . . are undesirable and not in line with the projected plan."[7]

What all of this really means is that the body is an effect, not a cause. It is an outpicturing of consciousness but without a life of its own. It is not a principle and does not have the power to impel, initiate, or become ill—only consciousness does. Therefore the body can be maintained in ideal condition through the primary intention of higher mind when we are on that frequency.

I think I've intuited a degree of this truth since I was a child. When I was six years old my mother dropped me off one early afternoon at the local movie house for a cowboy picture. It must have been my first western because I stayed in the theater hiding under the seats between showings until the place closed late that night. My mother almost had to be hospitalized. Even the sheriff and his deputies were looking for me—I could see them walking up and down the aisles all afternoon. The reason I didn't want to leave is that

I couldn't understand why they were showing the cowboys being killed by bullets. I remember thinking, "That can't happen. No matter what is done to a body, it can heal itself. People have forgotten how to be indestructible."

Perhaps I had tapped into some ancient memory that reminded me that mind is constantly creating a body—and you can't kill mind. Could we say that someday, when the collective consciousness is cleared of the Dweller energies, even the physical body cannot be harmed by bullets or bombs?

The physical body is a receptacle receiving its energy from consciousness. It is an instrument of the mind, a means of communication on the third-dimensional plane. We *have* a body, but we are not a body. In *Discipleship in the New Age, Volume I,* we read: "One of the problems which all sincere disciples have to solve, is to learn to live as if the physical body did not exist."[8] And *A Course in Miracles* tells us, "Freedom must be impossible as long as you perceive a body as yourself. The body is a limit. Who would seek for freedom in a body looks for it where it can not be found. The mind can be made free when it no longer sees itself as in a body, firmly tied to it and sheltered by its presence."[9]

The key is to keep our minds off the body and let it be vital and well through *consciousness* until our

Divine Self decides it is time to leave this plane of existence. In the meantime, what about the aging process? We are pure energy and energy does not ripen; the Essence of Being is forever removed from mutation. Every minute nature replaces the units of Life shining into the body as cells to provide us the occasion to begin anew, yet mind ages the energy to correspond to the age of mind. The secret of youthfulness is to be detached as much as possible from the race mind that believes in deterioration and decay and become young in consciousness. *Do everything for the joy of it!*

As we leave the physical system and move further inward, let's etch these truths in mind:

The Divine Self is the energy of Wholeness. It is the Principle of a perfect body. It is a misunderstanding of the Truth of Being that has resulted in illness. What is right understanding? That there is only one Mind—God. My essential Self is this Mind. There is no other mentality. What seems to be a personal mind is only a false belief in consciousness, the false belief that says Cause is in the physical form.

What I see as substantial is only a symbol of the reality behind it. The symbol does not have the power to give wellness. If I look to the symbol as real, its unstable nature will tell me of infirmity. If I dwell on the only Cause within, the harvest of health will be mine.

As above, so below. As within, so without. As I thinketh, I am. I know my Master Self indwelling as me lives in a state of eternal perfection, and I feel that truth in my heart. As above, so below. As I realize the truth of perfect being in my heart, I am healed. As within, so without.

God is perfect life. There is only one life. My life is God's life. Therefore, my life is perfect—without possibility of flaw, defect, blemish, or impairment. This is the Law. I see myself as God sees me, as God sees God in expression.

6

ENTERING THE ETHERIC RING

The next step inward is the etheric body, an energy blueprint of the physical system. It is composed of seven chakras (from Hindu, meaning spinning wheels of force) or energy centers that correspond to the physical body in a line from the head to the base of the spine. The physical counterparts to these etheric centers are the seven glands which created the body.

Why is it important to know about the etheric web? Because it is the transmitter of energy into the physical vehicle, and if it is devitalized the physical condition is affected. Remember, we want to be fit and hearty as we continue on the journey to the Infinite

Cause of all things good—so a quick review of the energy centers and glands is important at this juncture.

The center in the etheric energy above the top of the head (also called the crown chakra) corresponds to the pineal gland, and releases the energy of Will. This endows us with a sense of purpose in life and a stronger vitality to shield the body from disease before it enters. If this center is not functioning properly, the Will aspect is diminished and self-pity arises, a contributing factor to disease. Remedy: Be continuously more dedicated to a life purpose. Daily be inspired— even if you have to march through the house yelling "Be inspired, I *am* inspired! . . . Be inspired, I *am* inspired!" until the energy of inspiration starts pulsating in consciousness. Then meditate with feeling on these words:

> *The energy of inspiration is flowing freely through me now, infusing me with the fire of dynamic creativity and the driving motivation to fulfill my true purpose in life.*

The etheric center near the brow (third eye) relates to the pituitary gland and expresses the imagination. Downward visioning produces emotional upheavals and causes imbalance in the etheric. Depression follows, which weakens the nervous, circulatory, and respiratory systems. Remedy: Right use of imagination and harmlessness in all intentions. Live *as if* the spiritual nature is in full control and see only the good in life. This may have to be practiced daily for a time to correct old habits of visualizing negative scenes of "what might happen." When one of those scenarios comes to mind, say over and over:

My vision is fixed only on the greatest and grandest in life. Only my highest good is in expression at every moment in time and space.

The throat center and thyroid maintains the body's equilibrium in a state of well-being. If overactive, nervousness results which disturbs the body's metabolism. If underactive, there is no vitality of mind and body. Remedy: An attitude of open-mindedness. When one is opinionated and obstinate, creative energy is restricted. Also watch wrong use of power and selfish motives.

I seek spiritual understanding in all that I think, speak, and do. I speak only constructive words, and I use my power only for the greater good of all.

The heart center and thymus operating at proper tone stimulates the flow of energy and goodwill. If overactive, we are unable to distinguish between right and wrong, leading to irresponsibility. There will also be a forced concentration on trying to change the material world, to have an effect, without first a change in consciousness. On the reverse side, we tend to be withdrawn, distant, uncommunicative, beset by a sense of futility. In both instances the heart and circulatory system are vulnerable. Remedy: Greater feelings of Self-love (love directed to the higher Presence within) and unconditional love toward ourselves (the personality) and all others.

Love is the Essence of my Being. I love my Essence and recognize that it is one with all that is throughout creation. Love is the only power at work in my life, and I love everyone and everything without conditions.

The solar plexus center and pancreas form the instrument through which emotional energy flows. Most physical ailments are caused by a disturbance in this center due to wrong or selfish desires related to fear, guilt, anger, and resentment. If the emotions are in turmoil, a flood of negative energy flows through the solar plexus center and into the pancreas, adversely affecting the stomach, liver, gall bladder, and the entire nervous system. Remedy: Total forgiveness of self and others, a practice of unconditional love, and the understanding that the only Power to affect you is within—and it is eternally loving and good, never judging.

> I totally forgive myself for every thought, feeling, word, and deed of the past. As I forgive myself I am forgiving all, for I am everyone and everyone is me—and through the cleansing action of forgiveness, we are all wonderfully free.

The sacral center and gonads provide the energy of the sex life. In its natural state it fosters a powerful impulse toward fusion, which on the physical plane we call sexual intercourse, and our sex life becomes freer and more fulfilling. On the nonphysical level it is the urge for union with the Divine Part of us, the instinct toward unity with the Higher Self within. The gonads produce hormones which are indispensable to a healthy body. Maladies of the sexual organs are frequently the result of overstimulation of the sacral center through out-of-control desires, being out of balance in sexual energy. Conversely, some forms of cancer are the result of an inhibition of this natural desire. This repression sends shock waves into the emotional system, which can cause a disruption of cellular life. Remedy: A greater striving toward proper balance in all aspects of living, a choosing of the right course of action through a careful weighing of values.

I recognize and approve of myself and all others as spiritual beings temporarily clothed in physical form, and I joyfully accept my sexuality as part of the natural process of life. I love my (masculinity/femininity).

The base of the spine center and the corresponding adrenals produce a large number of hormones to help us handle stress. When the energy of this center is restricted, we feel physically exhausted, which lowers our resistance to disease. Remedy: To understand the difference between illusion and reality. The world of form is illusion because it is temporary. The eternal Reality is within—the true nature of being. Cease worrying about the nonessential things of life. Live fully, joyfully, dynamically.

My Divine Consciousness is expressing and manifesting as every good and perfect activity of my life, and there is nothing to fear today, tomorrow, or forever. The Light of Truth goes before me to dispel the shadows and reveal only that which is real in life—the divine order and harmony eternally existing in my world.

With the energy centers of the etheric moving into proper balance, we can now enter the astral plane, the sea of emotions swirling all around us. As we do, let's remember to keep the torch of joy burning brightly.

7

THE SEA OF
EMOTIONS ON
THE ASTRAL
PLANE

I want to preface our trip into the murky waters of the emotional system by saying that behind every problem is the shadow of a relationship. How do emotions and relationships tie together? You know the answer—it is difficult to have one without the other.

Unless handled lovingly, intelligently, and with great understanding, relationships with anyone from a chance encounter on the street to the closest family member can bring forth a negative emotional response, which shifts consciousness onto the astral plane where every sick, weird, ignorant, demented, hostile, and depraved pocket of energy exists.

The astral plane is the primary dwelling place of

the collective emotions of the human race. Every fear, hate, and trauma since the world began is there—all outpicturing in a dark fog of confusion and desperation. Individually we're a part of this fog. It is the basic energy of our egos fed into—and drawn back from—the Dweller Archetype. And it sets up a current around us that moves into intense vibration whenever we enter into a relationship.

Ageless Wisdom calls this astral energy the "veil of Isis," and the Bible refers to it as the Red Horse in the Four Horsemen of the Apocalypse. We also know it to be the Maze, the Wilderness, and the Great Illusion—and when we swing into it we have entered what the ancients called "impenetrable disorder." And it is this disorder that is responsible for sickness, financial insufficiency, unsatisfactory work, and an unfulfilled life.

We only have to go back to the Garden of Eden to find our symbolic starting point. It was *astral energy*—man's emotional nature—that tempted Adam in the allegory and not some woman called Eve. And since then essentially every problem the world has known can be traced back to that one word: *relationship*.

Consider how many people today blame someone else for their problems—husband, wife, father, mother, brother, sister, son, daughter, employer, employees, bankers, lawyers, men or women in general, a certain race or religion, the government, liberals, conservatives, elected officials, the courts, law enforcement, the IRS, the United Nations, extraterrestrials . . .

What do we do, become hermits and avoid relationships? We can't. Even alone on a desert island we would continue to relate to ourselves—to ego, our past lives, our shadow side, lower mind, higher mind, God. So the answer must be to transmute our emotional energy until it collectively dissolves, which the Wisdom teachings say will happen when the collective mind moves into a higher frequency. And we do this by working with *Light*, but first let's distinguish between emotions and feelings.

Emotions are *reactive*. They are in opposition to the natural process and represent our negative reaction in the form of anger, fear, guilt, desperation, jealousy, etc., to outside influences. Feelings on the other hand are *proactive*—acting in the affirmative, on the positive side, as in sensations of love, joy, peace, gratitude, and trusting. Our objective is to transmute negative emotions into positive feelings.

WORKING WITH THE LIGHT TO DISPEL THE ASTRAL FOG

First, let's determine which form of astral energy we're most vulnerable to. Perhaps a checklist of ten fog-based tendencies is appropriate at this point. (Check

the ones that apply specifically to you, and add others
that may come to mind.)

❏ *Unforgiveness.* I have tried to forgive, but I continue to hold resentment toward *(name the person,
authority figure, etc., referring to the partial list of
"relationships" noted earlier if necessary)*:

_____

_____

❏ *Fear.* My greatest fear is:

_____

_____

❏ *Discouragement.* I find myself frequently discour-
aged because of:

_____

_____

❏ *Unworthiness.* I don't feel worthy enough to have:

_____

_____

in my life at this time.

❏ *Futility.* Regardless of how hard I try to live the spiritual life, I still come up empty in the areas of:

_____

_____

❏ *All-consuming desire.* I am so strongly focused on *(name the effect):*

_____

_____

that I am unable to let go and let Cause express in my life.

❏ *Pridefulness.* The service I have embarked on "to make the world a better place" has made me self-centered, arrogant, pompous, *(add to the list):*

_____

_____

_____

_____

❑ *Selfish love.* I express affection to these people primarily to evoke the feeling of love from them:

_____

_____

❑ *Illusionary idealism.* I feel that my spiritual growth and personal happiness can best be achieved through my devotion to *(name the person, teacher, or other physical authority in physical form)*:

_____

_____

❑ *Criticism.* I feel it is all right to criticize *(name)*:

_____

because

_____

_____

Now let's go to work to release the Light. First, try to sense, see, and know that your emotional body—the astral plane projecting where you are—is hovering like a dark cloud all around you. Do not fear it. It is only a thought-form and only has the power we give it. We are taking away the power, but it doesn't know that.

Go into meditation and gently contemplate the infinite Knowingness, Love, Will, and Power of the One Self, the very Spirit of God individualized as you. Feel the overshadowing Presence and *love* that you are feeling. Remain there for several minutes receiving the love being poured out to you.

Now with your mind's eye see the brilliant blazing Light of this Holy Self permeating your entire being. Your Life Force is Light. Your energy body is Light. Your conscious awareness is filled with Light. All there is is Light. Bring the Light into your mind. You are a Mind of Light—a powerful searchlight of incredible brightness. See, feel, and know this.

Then with purpose of mind and a feeling of great love in your heart, begin to beam the Light into your emotional body, starting above the top of your head. This would be in the 12:00 position on a clock. Let the beam of light swing to your right, and see it slowly move counterclockwise around the circle. As it does, say aloud, "*Through the Power of the Healing Light, I now dispel the fog of* (whatever you checked on the list)." And keep repeating the words all around the circle.

Knowing that energy follows thought, see with the inner vision the Light penetrating the darkness, the thought-forms of emotional charges breaking up and dissolving. Let the Light circle your emotional field three times, while you continue to speak the words. Finally, see only Light around you, and accept the idea that an emotional healing has taken place.

When you have completed the process, express your gratitude to the Light of Spirit and go about your business. If old hurts and wounds seem to resurface, go through the circle of Light again three times, speaking the appropriate words. It is also helpful to remind yourself several times a day . . .

I live and move and have my being in Light. I am the Light unto my world, both inner and outer. Wherever I am at this moment is only Light, and darkness cannot enter.

In the Light we can experience all relationships with the fullness of joy and unconditional love.

8

THE MENTAL REALM

As we move into mind we are entering that aggregation of energy in closest proximity to the overshadowing light of our Divine Consciousness. It is the faculty of reasoning and active intelligence, and consciousness uses this energy in the manifestation of form.

You may ask, are not consciousness and mind the same thing? Not really. An individual's consciousness is a stream of divine awareness, understanding, and knowledge radiating as light from our spiritual nature through the mental, emotional, and etheric systems and connecting with the physical brain. Where consciousness is concentrated primarily—in the mental or emotional natures—determines the type of person we are. Unfortunately, only a small percentage of the population functions on the mental level. The majority of people, from the standpoint of personality, are emotional sponges, responding primarily to emotional stimulation.

As the light passes through these energy fields it is "colored" by the mental and emotional processes at work at any given time. Therefore, the light in expression as consciousness may well be adulterated by false beliefs and error patterns built up over a lifetime. This is why our initial focus was on the physical body—to pay less attention to it and more to consciousness. By moving above the body, so to speak, we're letting it be simply a reflection of consciousness. The next step inward was to the etheric to clear and balance our energies through right understanding, and then to the astral plane or emotional body to transmute our reactive thought-forms and bring peace to the raging sea. Now we want to heal the mental sphere so that the light has a clear passage for optimal expression through our fields of energy. In essence, we want our Divine Consciousness to shine through into expression and manifestation with as few impediments as possible.

The purpose of our personal minds is to be an agent of the Divine Self, a transmitter of the highest and finest energy. When the physical body is filled with this higher energy, conditions of disease will not exist. The fact that there is so much sickness in this world is a direct reflection of the average person's failure to use his or her mind. Most people do not think—their thoughts think them—and this is why the mind must be disciplined.

It is interesting though that few human problems are caused by mind or negative thinking. Disease, suffering, turmoil, discord, failure, and poverty are the result of restricting the flow of spiritual energy, and the mind is the first reservoir to receive this energy. If the mind is in a mode of fanaticism or unbridled zealotry, the energy is overstimulated and may adversely affect the nervous system. Attitudes that are contrary to the principle of love and goodwill will contaminate the energy and become a catalyst for undesirable emotional reactions as the energy enters that force field. A downward visioning mind bonded with the emotional system simply releases the light *to be wounded in accordance with its prevalent wounds.*

Dr. Douglas Baker, English author and teacher of Ancient Wisdom, has written that, "The mental body should be in control of the other two (physical and astral bodies) and consciousness should, therefore be mentally polarised. All matters of the day should be dealt with at a mental (not emotional) level. The resulting poise produced will reflect itself in the personality which would then be stable and (if not already so) tending towards complete integration. It will be wide open to new ideas, concepts, disciplines, priorities, senses or value without being unstable."[1]

Let's never forget that love is a quality of mind and not the emotions. When the mind is clear we can love unconditionally. Also, intuition is a function of the mind, not the emotional nature. When the mind is open our guidance from within comes forth with great clarity. This clearing and opening of mind begins with a deeper understanding of energy, followed by cleansing, control, and coordination.

TRAINING THE MIND TO IDENTIFY WITH ENERGY

The mind is pure energy. When it begins to associate with energy it begins to awaken to its true nature. *Think* now as you read about this awesome force and power.

All there is throughout the universe and beyond, in every dimension and in all levels of being, is *energy*. And what we know as an "individual" is a state of energy-consciousness sustained in a whirlpool of energies—a force field of life, intelligence, and power. Each one of us is an individualization of the sum-total of all energies, or that which we know as God. Unless we realize this, we will continue to live with a succession of false identities in mind.

We may be as hypnotized children who have exchanged our minds for the will, doctrine, and dictatorial beliefs of others, without hope of a carefree, joyous, and fulfilling life in the present moment. Or we may be like rebellious adolescents who also live in a state of hopelessness caught up in folly, deceit, manipulation, and crime. Then there are the "good people"—those seemingly mature individuals who go through life in a state of unawareness about anything other than the body—the physical body and its sensations, the family body and its obligations, the church body and its rules of salvation, the job body and its limitations, and the government body and its perceived power. I use the word "body" to refer to *effects*—the systems, units, structures, and things "out there" where power is given away and the person becomes the slave and victim of an outer authority.

The next identity that we may assume is one who sees the infinite possibilities in life, not in the present tense but always in the future. While in this state of mind happiness is always geared to the days, months, and years ahead—for the right mate to be found, the next promotion to be won, the money to come, the health to improve, life to get easier. We live in the past while projecting our hopes and wishes down the road into the never-never land of Tomorrow, and then run like crazy trying to catch the dream before time runs out.

Then at some point in our evolution we begin to be aware of the light shining from within, and we commence the inner journey back to the awakened state. And in the process we find that there are various *frequencies* in consciousness, and that our phenomenal world reflects perfectly the frequency we are on at the moment. Soon we realize that these frequencies relate specifically to levels of energy, and finally we come to understand that the identity of that energy-force is *I AM*—the concentrated focus of the Energy of the Infinite eternally expressing as every form and experience in life.

Do you understand what this means? Not only is God everywhere present as the sum-total of all energies unformed and formed, but we are the energy of all that exists in our personal worlds. From the invisible to the visible all is energy, first as pure light, then as lines of force, next as patterns of energy, and finally as the form itself. In reverse we see the form, the pattern holding the energy in form, the lines of force holding the pattern, and back up into the original energy of light. As we practice this exercise with rocks, plants, animals, people—everything animate and inanimate—we are training the mind to think as energy.

Ponder these thoughts:

I am consciously aware of the dynamic energy force that I Am. I understand that there is nothing but energy behind all form and in

*every experience, and I live steadily in the light
of that understanding. I know that I am pure
energy, that I live and move and have my
being in omnipresent energy, and I continuously practice this idea of seeing and knowing
the forces of energy at work.*

CLEANSING THE MENTAL BODY

In my book *The Angels Within Us* I talked about ban-
ishing mental illusions caused by misperception and
misunderstanding through the use of symbols. I wrote,
"By concentrating on a symbol you penetrate beyond
its surface appearance and come to realize its subjec-
tive reality. Such an exercise will give you a grasp of
the underlying idea of the symbol, its meaning and sig-
nificance, and through practice you will begin to
understand the actual energy vibration of the symbol.
It will seem to tell you about itself. Symbol meditation
will clear the cobwebs from your mind and bring your
immediate personal world into sharper focus, enabling
you to be in greater control of your life. The seven
most-used symbols for meditation are the circle, the
triangle, the square, the circle squared, the lens sphere,
the cube, and the pyramid."[2]

I think it's best to bring the images of the symbols
to mind rather than focusing on a piece of art. This
can lead to self-hypnosis and general disorientation
rather than an ordering of mind for greater soundness.

Another exercise used in the ancient sacred academies to cleanse the mental body was the "divine alchemy of fire." It is a technique utilizing the energy of the various astrological sun signs, and can be very effective in burning away the dregs of mind—based on the principle that energy follows thought. Remember that the sun sign indicates the date of your birth: ARIES, March 21–April 19; TAURUS, April 20–May 20; GEMINI, May 21–June 21; CANCER, June 22–July 22; LEO, July 23–August 22; VIRGO, August 23–September 22; LIBRA, September 23–October 22; SCORPIO, October 23–November 21; SAGITTARIUS, November 22–December 21; CAPRICORN, December 22–January 19; AQUARIUS, January 20–February 18; PISCES, February 19–March 20.

A modified version of the exercise is as follows:

> *Let the aspirant whose sun sign is Capricorn, Taurus, or Virgo bring in the cosmic fire at the Sacral Chakra.* (Located opposite the navel on the etheric spinal column.)
>
> *Let the aspirant whose sun sign is Pisces, Cancer, or Scorpio bring in the cosmic fire at the Solar Plexus Chakra.*
>
> *Let the aspirant whose sun sign is Aquarius, Gemini, or Libra bring in the cosmic fire at the Throat Chakra.*
>
> *Let the aspirant whose sun sign is Aries,*

Leo, or Sagittarius bring in the cosmic fire at the Third Eye Chakra.

Wherever the fire originates, O Seeker of Truth, see it burning as a mighty cleansing flame. Feel the heat. Let it ascend up through the Crown Chakra, and with the inner eye follow the fire. Dive upward into the flame!

Now O Seeker of True Vision, see with the inner eye the setting sun in the western sky and let the Spiritual Sun set in your mind. Hold your mind steady in the light of the Shining Sun.

Now O Seeker of Wholeness, feel the force of love from the Master Sun within radiate through your mind. Focus your mind on the Light of the One Self through contemplative meditation.

Another way to cleanse the mental body of an ineffectual and helpless state of mind is to think of ourselves as electromagnetic fields of energy—*electrically activated magnetism,* which relates specifically to the law of attraction and the principle of atomic affinity. Ageless wisdom tells us that "The fire of mind is fundamentally electricity"[3]—and science has known for centuries that everything that exists is composed of atoms with electrons and protons, the negative and positive particles of electricity. One of the early teachings was that the entire universe is a manifestation of electrical power, and that the laws of thought and the laws of electricity are based on the same principle. Let's not forget that even though the word "electricity" was not coined until 1646, the early theories about electricity were discussed hundreds of years before the birth of Jesus.

Electricity is not a source of power but rather a form of energy. Electric current follows a circuit and functions on the basis of polarity as it establishes a magnetic field around the circuit. Similarly, the radiation from the Central Core of our being is electrical power, and this flowing current sets up a magnetic field around our thoughts to form a circuit. However, when our thoughts are not in tune with our Higher Mind, the circuit is not complete because there is no magnetic attraction or polarity. To say it another way, attunement with our Core Reality releases an electrical current of essentially infinite power—and our thoughts become high circuits for the power, which aligns us with the Angel Archetype. But when our thoughts emanate from the lower vibration of our energy field we are in direct parallel with the friction fire of the race mind and the Dweller Archetype. At this level our low thoughts become openings in consciousness through which the Dweller energy manifests a lower quality of life.

When we think of ourselves as shining lights and radiating power centers, our energy is in constant movement. Accordingly, we should have a point of association to frequently remind us of the high-voltage power plants that we are, and this can be the electrical power that we live with daily. Let's rid our minds of powerless thoughts by being consciously aware of the mighty electrical power within us, the circuits that right thinking develops, the currents that are constantly flowing out—and let this awareness be triggered every time we see a light burning, turn on a light, use an appliance, switch on a radio or television, call someone on the telephone, or start our cars.

In truth we are electromagnetic fields filled with divine circuits that are manifesting perfection in our lives. And when we turn off a light let's remember that the electricity is still there, waiting to be used for a specific purpose through the flick of a switch—just as the Power flowing through us responds to the magnetic attraction of our right thoughts.

Controlling the Mind

The mind is controlled through concentration and visualization, but the concentration here is different than that discussed with the symbols, for now the mental application will be on animation.

In his book *The Phoenix*, Manly Hall writes, "Concentration is simply the pointing of mental effort, the focusing of the mind so that the object of attention shall be an undivided interest. Concentration involves the coordination of the intellectual parts under the dominion of the will, the function of the will being to contribute intensity and continuity to mental effort. The average person has poor continuity. He cannot carry a train of thought to its logical destination. In other words, he cannot think things through. . . . The purpose of concentration is to begin the organization of the mental powers so that the mind actually becomes that which it was designed to be—an instrument for the discernment of relative values and realities."[4]

Hall suggests we begin by the contemplation of action, such as visualizing a beautiful rose and the opening of its bud. "Having chosen some such appropriate figure, the mind should be given the task of envisioning it and the practice continued until the image can be invoked at pleasure and held an indefinite period of time. . . . The flower should be envisioned as about two feet in front of the face, hanging as it were in space, and after the concentration is sufficient to retain it there, the blossom may be given animation, opening from a bud to a full blown state."[5]

I have also used this exercise to image in my mind a seed becoming a tree, a child in fast-forward development becoming an adult, a blank piece of paper suddenly transformed into a book. It's a marvelous way to stretch the mind and improve the continuity of thought.

COORDINATING THE MENTAL BODY WITH THE FOUR HIGHER ENERGY CENTERS

Whereas the emotional system relates directly to the solar plexus, sacral, and base of spine chakras, the mental body is associated with the crown, third eye, throat, and heart centers, which in turn control will, insight, creative power, and love. To affect a healthy relationship between mind and its etheric centers, *think* as clearly as possible while answering these questions:

1. What do I consider the Divine Will for my life?
2. What do I see as the real purpose in my life?
3. How can this purpose best be manifested and what can I do to assist in bringing this plan into form and experience?
4. How can I, as just one man or woman, provide a true service to this world?

Through your answers to these questions, which may be modified over time, the mental body will begin its coordination process. The energy of the head chakra will focus on will, leading to your primary intention in life. The energy of the third eye will focus on insight, leading to a higher vision of your purpose for being. The energy of the throat center will focus on creative power, leading to a higher degree of creative intelligence in mind. And the energy of the heart chakra will focus on love, leading you to a greater understanding of your plan of service. As the energies of the mental body blend, your mind will be in a state of higher coordination.

Now meditate in a focused contemplation on the meaning of these four statements:

I WILL.
I SEE.
I CREATE.
I LOVE.

As you have probably guessed, the training, cleansing, controlling, and coordinating of the mind is for one specific purpose: to become a transparency for the light of spirit. Scientist Orest Bedrij says that to find our Creator, "it is crucial that *the mind be still* and that *the heart be loving and pure.* Note that a mere knowledge of food does not help a hungry person. Similarly, it is not enough to know intellectually the principles of purity of heart or stillness of mind. They must be experienced directly if we are to perceive who we are."[6]

By following the suggested action in Part II of this book, and opening yourself to further guidance from within, the purification of heart and the removing of unruly chatter from mind has begun. The vibration of your entire energy field has changed, enabling you to cross the bridge into the Fourth Dimension—the Land of All and Is. It is a vast region of goodness, truth, and beauty where all that we could ever seek in life exists in infinite abundance.

Let's hurry. There's so much to see and experience.

PART III

LIVING THE
SPIRITUAL
LIFE

9

LIVING
WITH LOVE

As we cross into the New Land let's be consciously
aware that all of the dimensions of the universe
are *frequencies*, a sliding scale of oneness from the
level of form reaching all the way to the highest vibration of pure energy. Thus, at this point in our journey
we are simply entering a new and higher frequency of
being—and we see now how we can live joyfully in the
third dimension with a physical body while our consciousness is in the fourth and beyond. It is a uniting
of heaven and earth, the invisible and visible. And we
should note that the fruits of our lives are a direct indi-
cation of what frequency we're operating on—the
outer reflects the inner.

To move into those higher frequencies and *remain* there, we must understand what it means to live in and with love. Unfortunately, many people can't even define the word. If someone says, "I love you," what is he or she saying? On one level it is nothing more than "I desire your body"—and moving up from there the interpretations might be "I desire your heart and mind" . . . "I desire your energy" . . . "I desire your friendship" . . . "I desire your spirit to be one with mine in an eternal bonding."

> *"Love," Thomas Aquinas writes, "is naturally the first act of the will and appetite; for which reason all the other appetitive movements presuppose love, as their root and origin. For nobody desires anything nor rejoices in anything, except as a good that is loved."*[1]

So we see that love in personal relationships does draw on the emotion of desire, which in a true bonding situation is then transformed into *giving* without demands rather than selfish *getting*—a "wish to act for the good of the beloved, as well as in its wish to be loved in return."[2]

Even "the oldest book in the world" talks about acting for the good of the beloved. *The Precepts of Ptah-Hotep* written three thousand years before Jesus by a 110-year-old Egyptian teacher—said to be the world's earliest known author—tells us to "love thy wife without allow. Caress her, fulfill her desires during the time of her existence . . . behold to what she aspires, at what she aims, what she regards. Open thy arms for her, respondent to her arms; call her, display to her thy love."[3]

An excellent instruction from five thousand years ago. But can we really love anyone else until we first love ourselves? The Bible tells us to first love our true nature and then everyone else as that spiritual self. So love does begin with how we look upon ourselves.

Take a moment and think about who and what you are. What is there not to love? The body? Love it as your communications vehicle on the physical plane and your love will maintain the visible form in the energy of love. The personality? Love it and watch how it changes to mirror that love. The Divine Consciousness of your essential Self? That's the full embodiment of universal love—the very Self-expression of God. Can you not love God expressing as you? You are a great, grand, magnificent being, the sum-total of all the cosmic energies individualized as the being you are. Love the completeness of yourself, then turn your gaze to the one closest to you and see another *super-*being, and continue the rollout of your vision until you see everyone as the very Selfhood of God in individual expression.

I believe that Jan and I have enjoyed being who we are since childhood, which certainly helped in the uniting of our souls. Sure we've had arguments, but something happened during our first year of marriage that put a seal of love on our relationship. One day after fuming and yelling at each other for an hour we suddenly started laughing. She said, "Why in the world did we do that? We love each other so much."

And I said, "Tell you what. From now on, any time either of us starts to get testy with the other let's speak a magic word to dispel the cloud."

"What magic word?"

I thought for a moment, then said, "Rowr."

"Rowr? What does it mean?"

I said, "It's just a made-up word that means we love each other too much and life is too short to waste away with silly fights. So we'll speak the word whenever it's necessary and laugh at our foolishness."

She agreed and the next day I had an artist make a large cardboard sign with the word "Rowr" and we had it framed. Later the word became so important to us that we began to call each other *Rowr*—and still do. We know now that its true meaning is love.

Let's continue on for an even deeper understanding of this most mysterious quality of life. To do this we have to go all the way back to "the beginning."

As I pointed out in *The Planetary Commission*, "Love is what created the universe, and Love is what the universe was created out of. Therefore, Love is Mind and also the thoughts of Mind. Love is the thrust of all creation. 'And God said . . .' And the Word was Love . . . and the Power of the Word was Love . . . and the manifestation of the Power was Love. All *is* Love!"[4]

All is love. Love is light, love is energy, love is substance, love is the creative power behind all manifestation. "Remember that money is the consolidation of the loving, living energy of divinity, and that the greater the realization and expression of love, the freer will be the inflow of that which is needed to carry forward the work."[5]

We live and move and have our being in the energy of love. We breathe love, our bodies are sustained by love, and our Life Force is pure love. We can't get out of love—it's omnipresent. We can't out-think love—it's omniscient, and as it's omnipotent, we can't overpower it. It is the single force of universal Cause and its permanent home is within each one of us. We are eternally the fire and flame of divine love burning brightly, the light of God-love shining throughout every dimension. I AM perfect love is the truth of the ages.

Love is law or principle in action—not only spiritual laws but also the laws of physics. The nucleus of the *atom* is pure love as is the central core of each individual and all of nature. And everything that exists is made up of love atoms. We live in a world of love and it responds to us through this recognition and understanding. The kinetic energy called *heat* is love—just think of the soothing warmth in a loving relationship. Can an icy personality attract warmheartedness?

Love as *light* travels in waves and can harmonize situations in the twinkling of an eye. Jan knows this, and when a neighbor dog began to regularly knock over the garbage can and litter the street she took care of the situation. The next time the garbage was taken out she circled the container with love and we both stood back and watched. In a few minutes the dog came down the street and ran right smack into that love energy. He quickly turned away and never again bothered the garbage. Love protects. Love guards. Love calms. Love restores.

We frequently radiate love energy to the sales clerks during the busy holiday season, to waiters in crowded restaurants, and to cab drivers. It's beautiful to see the cold, sour expressions turn warm and pleasant.

Jan was on a radio show in San Francisco, and upon its completion the producer called a cab for us. As we entered the car we silently showered love on the driver and asked him to take us to our hotel. On the way he asked what we were doing at the station. Jan told him and showed him a copy of her book. He asked, "Did you learn anything over there?" She gave him a brief report, and when we arrived at the hotel I reached into my wallet to pay the tab. He shook his head, saying, "No charge." He looked back at Jan and said, "To use an old expression, you made my day." I think the message of love from her book did it.

Love in action is *magnetism* and draws love to us wherever we are. When we are *being* love in consciousness we attract goodwill, helpfulness, and loving support from everyone—and we seem to be invisible to others with a negative, hostile vibration. In truth, love attracts love.

In the chapter on relationships in *Angel Energy* I told about how a friend in Dallas drew the perfect man to her. After my book was published she wrote an article for the *Quartus Report* to further explain the method used. Here are some excerpts:

> *I got busy. Now I had gotten busy before, mind you. I had visualized, fantasized, treasure mapped and tried all of the other metaphysical goings on in order to bring my dreams into reality. Why hadn't they worked? I know now—I was leaving out the most important yet easiest step: What I wanted for myself I had to see for everyone else. It was that simple. This program won't work if you can see a Marriage Made in Heaven for yourself, but not for your enemies.*[6]

The "program" consisted of several steps including the statement: "My intention is to be a clear and open channel for the full expression of a Marriage Made in Heaven in my life"—followed by an acceptance of that energy, a radiation of the energy throughout her world, the visualization of her new husband as a pillar of light and the wedding ceremony down to the last detail, and the expression of gratitude for what was sure to come. She also spoke these words: "That which I decree for myself, I decree for all according to each soul's choice and acceptance."

What started happening in my life once I began this process is amazing. Several times a day I radiated the light energy of a Marriage Made in Heaven to every person where I worked. Then I started radiating this energy to every person on the street, and to every blip in my consciousness. For example, I used to drive past several strip joints on my way to and from work, and was upset that these places existed. Now I was driving past them radiating the love energy of a Marriage Made in Heaven to every woman who worked there and to every man that frequented those hot spots. I realized that if we all were with the one person who loved us unconditionally, inspired us to be the best we could be, and we in turn did this for them, this would actually

lead to peace on earth. Now I really felt like
an Ambassador!
　　It only took three weeks before my man
(now my husband) appeared. We were married
a few months later. My life is magnificent!

There is nothing that love cannot do—but we must be aware of it, understand it, and *know* it. Then love takes control of the personality and we become a channel for the expression of God's love, the one power and presence in this universe. As minister-author Eric Butterworth wrote in *Life Is for Loving*, "When you are conscious that you are *in* love with life, with all God's creation, and that the whole universe is *in* love with you, you have everything going for you. You have the sense that you are 'destiny's darling,' that there are green lights wherever you look. This consciousness wells up from within you and you clap your hands with joy from the overflow."[7]

　　Let's live in love, with love, as love, maintaining the love vibration for every part of our being—from the tip of our nose all the way to the Self of Love within us and everyone else, and to the Father-Mother Love that created us out of love and eternally lives in love within that Self. When we are conscious of love, there is nothing but love in our lives—and we will indeed clap our hands with joy.

A MEDITATION

I choose to live with love.

If there has been any disharmony in my life, it shows me that I haven't loved enough, for love is the correcting principle of the universe. When I truly love and let it flow, it goes before me to straighten every crooked place.

The highest form of love is to love my Holy Self and the presence of God dwelling therein. My loving gaze at the Magnificence within releases the kingdom to come forth into my world. And I behold that all things are made new through love. I meditate on this.

As I quiet myself and look within, I see and feel the Mind of infinite love—the very presence of my Holy Self. The vibration is warm and soothing, and I have a sense of being lifted up, up, up into the Heart of eternal love.

In this presence I find joy and serenity. There is no mental effort now as I relax into the rhythm of God, into the celestial harmony. I am now in the Kingdom of Love, which I am told by the gentle voice from within is what I am.

WHAT I was seeking, I AM. And the voice speaks of my true nature, the spirit of the Living God in individual expression—totally loved and loving.

WHO I was seeking, I AM. I AM my Holy Self, and all that my Holy Self is, I AM, and all that my Holy Self has, is mine. My love is complete, and I go forth now to live in love, with love, as love.

10

LIVING WITH FORGIVENESS

In the Bhagavad Gita we are told that forgiveness is one of the "transcendental qualities born of the godly atmosphere."[1] And in the Bible Jesus reminds us that effective prayer always begins with forgiveness—"Forgive if you have anything against any one" (Mark 11:25).

"Forgiveness represents your function here,"[2] says *A Course in Miracles*, and continues with this vitally important instruction: *Forgive, and you will see this differently.* "These are the words the Holy Spirit speaks in all your tribulations, all your pain, all suffering regardless of its form. These are the words with which temptation ends, and guilt, abandoned, is revered no more. These are the words which end the dream of sin, and rid the mind of fear. These are the words by which salvation comes to all the world."[3]

As a transcendental quality, the key to prayer, the end of guilt and the method of salvation, forgiveness must be quite a transforming power. Conversely, *unforgiveness* can be likened to guck in a stopped up plumbing system. Look at it this way:

> If I feel anger, animosity, annoyance, displeasure, indignation, irritation, or jealousy toward anyone, I am in a state of unforgiveness, which dams the channels of spirit and blocks the creative energy.

The negative attributes mentioned above all relate to *resentment*, which is the original definition of unforgiveness. So to forgive, we "give up resentment against or the desire to punish; stop being angry with; pardon" (Webster). How do we do this? We begin by forgiving ourselves for all our miscreations. As I wrote in *The Angels Within Us* . . .

> Actually it really wasn't you who miscreated; it was a false belief, or thought-form, called ego which is nothing but a part of the great illusion in your life—yet ego-action can leave emotional wounds that must be healed. In forgiving yourself you are simply calling in

the Energy of Correction, the Law of Adjust-
ment, to transmute the old erroneous patterns
and eliminate the ghosts of another time.

Scan your consciousness, and if something
from your past comes up that triggers a feeling
of shame or self-condemnation, bring the
whole scenario into full view and cast the
entire memory-image upon the Love of God
within you. Do not attempt to push it farther
down out of mind. That is repression. Give it
up to Spirit and let it be burned away. Keep
pulling up all the old sin-fear-guilt roots and
tossing them on the Holy Fire within, and keep
at it until you feel clean and clear again.
Understand that it is impossible to release any
thought or feeling to Spirit for transmutation
without divine action taking place.[4]

Next we want to give up any form of resentment
toward anyone within the range of our consciousness.
This becomes easier when we realize that what we're
seeing in others (causing resentment in us) is nothing
more than a projection of our ego on them. We're
seeing something of ourselves that we don't like in the
other person. So even though he or she really has done
nothing for which to be forgiven (which is the way
God sees us), let's forgive our ego thoughts, the projection, and the person.

I choose to totally and completely forgive everyone and everything from the beginning of time right up to the present moment. If there is anyone I feel I cannot forgive—including myself—I forgive my unforgiveness and ask my Holy Self to forgive through me. I choose to be free of any and all resentment.

In my book *Angel Energy*, I wrote:

When we remember that everything is based on the law of cause and effect, we see again that it is our consciousness that produces the undesirable experiences in life. Eventually we arrive at the conclusion that the outer world is only secondary to the inner world of consciousness, and our focus begins to change from without to within. We reverse our attention and begin to look for the crossed wires in our system, the faulty circuits that are limiting the Great Unlimited. And when the obstructions and impediments are removed through forgiveness of the past and a deeper awareness of our spiritual nature, the ego's projected effects begin to fade and are simultaneously replaced with higher impressions of a more substantial nature.[5]

I have found it helpful to begin and end each day with forgiveness—giving up resentment toward anyone and everything that stirred my emotions in a negative way. And that would include politicians, religious zealots, columnists, talk show hosts on radio, the author of a particular book, a family member, my computer, a careless driver on the freeway, the planetary energies, the weather, the whole crazy world for not being what I want it to be—and above all myself. And I frequently remind myself of times past when things seemed to be "out of kilter" and were remedied through the simple act of silent forgiveness.

When I once forgave a debtor, the debt was quickly paid. A forgiven automobile suddenly began functioning properly. A forgiven financial situation resulted in a new manifestation of abundance. The critical attitude of a friend, when forgiven without words spoken, produced an outpouring of kindness. When we give *up* annoyance, aggravation, and irritation it is dissolved and the powerful process of the natural order of things immediately swings into action to reveal harmony. For example . . .

Jan and I were flying out of Los Angeles with only a forty-five-minute pad in Dallas to catch the flight to San Antonio. The plane was fifteen minutes late in backing away from the gate because one of the flight attendants said she heard a funny grinding noise in one of the engines.

There's no use worrying about anything, every-thing's just fine.

They checked the engine and the captain relayed the information from the flight deck that it was okay and we began moving toward the runway. As we were preparing for takeoff, a woman in the back had an anxiety attack and demanded that the plane return to the gate and let her off. It was contagious. Two other women sitting behind her said they wanted to get off too. So the plane headed back to the gate and we waited another thirty minutes for their luggage to be unloaded. Taxiing back to the runway Jan said, "We've used up over an hour. Guess we'd better call on the angels. Our dogs are expecting us on time."

To properly work with those Living Energies within requires a forgiving heart, so we both forgave everything related to the situation. Guess what? We were only ten minutes late arriving in Dallas and made our plane for San Antonio with plenty of time to spare.

A MEDITATION

I choose to live with forgiveness by refusing to feel resentment toward any person, place, situation, or thing. I give up any sense of ever being offended by anyone.

I cast all bitterness, hurts, and indignation upon the Holy Flame within, knowing that this energy will immediately be transformed by the Divine Fire. I do this now, knowing this is the true meaning of forgiveness.

11

LIVING WITH WISDOM

To live joyously in the light of our Divine Consciousness we must live with wisdom. In essence, wisdom is knowing what life is really all about. It's learning how to distinguish between the unreal and real, and how to live in harmony with all of creation. And the hallmark of wisdom is *simplicity*. Because true wisdom has a beautiful easiness about it—a straightforward clarity—many of us discount its great depth. We tend to think that only abstruse principles are worthy of our attention, yet consciousness expands to greater heights more quickly through the obvious.

When I think of teachings on attaining greater wisdom I am immediately drawn to the East and 500 B.C.—to the place and time of a man who has been called "the prince of philosophers, the wisest and most consummate of sages, the loftiest moralist, the most subtle and penetrating intellect that the world had ever seen."[1] His name was Confucius.

Scholar and translator Lionel Giles, Litt.D., said that the teaching of Confucius is "absolutely the purest and least open to the charge of selfishness of any in the world."[2] Perhaps the reason for this accolade is that the Chinese sage practiced what I call "spiritual common sense." He understood human nature—how our minds work—but he also knew that because of the innate goodness of each individual, life's experiences could be translated into harmony through a higher vision. A true metaphysician, he taught the language of Spirit without preaching a religion.

Let's see what we can learn from this wisest of sages, remembering that when he uses the masculine "man" he is referring to both genders. Here are a few excerpts from *The Analects of Confucius*. Ponder these greatly profound yet simple truths.

The higher type of man is one who acts before he speaks, and professes only what he practices. The nobler sort of man in his progress

*through the world has neither narrow predilec-
tions nor obstinate antipathies. What he follows is the line of duty.*

Before any action can take place, the thought must
precede it. We should *think* and then act, without first
running around and telling everyone what we're going
to do. That dissipates the energy and creates road-
blocks. Let's keep our intentions to ourselves as we
follow "the line of duty" (what we consider our purpose in this lifetime) and let the results of our efforts
do the talking for us. And we should only claim (pro-
fess) that which we can live up to, i.e., we "practice
what we preach." It is also important that our par-
tiality, love, and fondness (predilection) be inclusive
and unconditional, while willing to be more reasonable and flexible toward what we may dislike in others
and consider repugnant. This is being tolerant and
more understanding of others.

*True goodness springs from a man's own
heart. How can it depend on other men?*

All that is good, true, and beautiful in life must
come forth from within. When we are dependent on
the Holy Self for everything, we are working with true
Cause. When we rely on others for our good, we are
worshiping a false god. There is no power in the outer
world.

*What you would not wish done to yourself, do
not unto others.*

This is the very practical wisdom of the Golden
Rule, and if truly understood would dramatically
change our lives.

*The princely man is one who knows neither
grief nor fear. If on searching his heart he finds
no guilt, why should he grieve? Of what
should he be afraid?*

As Jan pointed out in her book *The Other Side of
Death*, "guilt demands punishment, the death penalty in
my case. . . ."[3] And since we believe in a sentence based
on the guilt we feel, we begin to fear the punishment, and
the fear brings grief. Jan was also told that when we can
forgive ourselves, the penalty is removed. Earlier we
talked about forgiveness but let's pause right now and
move up to that princely state of mind and tell ourselves
that we've never done anything wrong. Every thought,
word, and deed was simply a state of consciousness in
action, and that mind-set no longer exists. We're not the
same person we were even yesterday, and we can certainly forgive ourselves for the past and close that door.
When we remove the guilt there is nothing to be afraid of.

*The higher type of man seeks all that he wants
in himself; the inferior man seeks all that he*

*wants from others. The higher type of man is
firm but not quarrelsome; sociable, but not
clannish. The wise man does not esteem a
person more highly because of what he says,
neither does he undervalue what is said
because of the person who says it.*

The latter part of the teaching above concerning
the "wise man" is very important. Frequently, meaningful guidance in life comes from someone who we
may not consider even very intelligent, much less a
master of wisdom. As I wrote in *Practical Spirituality*,
"There is but one Guide, one Voice, yet It uses different channels to reach you depending on the vibration of your consciousness. And over the years I've
also met many men and women in physical form who
just happened to say something to me that opened my
mind and heart to a new understanding."[4]

*The nobler sort of man pays special attention
to nine points. He is anxious to see clearly, to
hear distinctly, to be kindly in his looks,
respectful in his demeanor, conscientious in his
speech, earnest in his affairs; when in doubt,
he is careful to inquire; when in anger, he
thinks of the consequences; when offered an
opportunity for gain, he thinks only of his duty*
(his purpose in life).

Let's think about a conversation we might be having with someone. Are we trying to see his or her point clearly without judging according to our own belief system? Are we really listening to what is being said rather than thinking ahead to what we want to say? Are we expressing kindness and respect in the way we're looking at the other person and in our body language? In every relationship we should watch what we say, be sincere, do what we can to avoid misunderstanding, and be true to our inner integrity—to ourSelves.

> *Moral virtue simply consists of being able, anywhere and everywhere, to exercise five particular qualities: Self-respect, magnanimity, sincerity, earnestness and benevolence.*

Let's think of "moral virtue" as the practice of being ethical and honorable from the highest state of mind. We reach this level through the proper regard and reverence for our True Self, and then treating everyone else with forgiveness, sincerity, thoughtfulness, and kindness. This is loving your Lord-Self and loving your neighbor as that Self.

> *If I am walking with two other men, each of them will serve as my teacher. I will pick out the good points of the one and imitate them,*

and the bad points of the other and correct them in myself.

Everyone is our teacher in one way or another.

All my knowledge is strung on one connecting thread.

The "connecting thread" is life, and to this great sage life was a journey of self-improvement and being true to himself.

Observe a man's actions; scrutinize his motives; take note of the things that give him pleasure. How, then, can he hide from you what he really is?

We are constantly onstage. To paraphrase Emerson, "What you are speaks so loudly I cannot hear what you say." The key here, however, is to observe ourselves, and when we do we realize that we can't hide from our character—that which we are expressing as a personality. Let's take stock of the kind of person we are and make the necessary adjustments.

Among the various things you hear said, reserve your judgment on those which seem doubtful, and give cautious utterance to the rest: Then you will seldom fall into error. Among the various things you see done, set aside those which seem dangerous, and cautiously put the others into practice: Then you will seldom have occasion for repentance. If you seldom err in your speech, and seldom have to repent of your actions, official preferment will come of itself.

Let's measure our spoken words carefully and use discernment in every action we take. Then the warranted advances (official preferment) in life will come naturally, as part of the *natural* process of living.

It is by observing a man's faults that one may come to know his virtues.

Each person is innately good. Even the defects of personality cannot hide the light of truth shining through when we look beyond the physical being. Let us acknowledge the true spiritual essence of everyone we encounter.

If you work for your own selfish ends, you will make many enemies.

Common sense—and true wisdom.

When you see a good man, think of emulating him; when you see a bad man, examine your own heart.

Another example of watching what we are unconsciously projecting on others. People will frequently mirror in speech and behavior what we have repressed—positively or negatively—about ourselves.

Fix the mind on truth; cling to virtue; give play to loving-kindness; recreate yourself with the arts.

The first three statements are part and parcel of living the spiritual life, and the last one emphasizes the transforming power of creative work. When we are involved in an activity that contributes to our personal perception of beauty, structure, tone, and movement, the mind is focused, emotions are stilled, the feeling nature enhanced, and we become a part of the cosmic dance—in the universal rhythm of order and harmony.

It is not easy to find a man who after three years of self-cultivation has not reached happiness.

"Self-cultivation" has also been translated from the Chinese to mean "self-learning"—and the point here is that it should take an individual only three years to reach that state of consciousness where happiness is an enduring experience. What about the people who have devoted years to the study of truth principles and still for the most part are joyless and discontented? The simple fact is that they haven't learned anything. In my book *Practical Spirituality* I told the story of the man from India who asked an American missionary to tell him about his religion.

The American said, "Well, it's really based on a prayer given to us by Jesus."

"And what is this prayer?"

The missionary replied, "Our Father . . ." But before he could say anything else the Indian vanished into the crowd.

A few years later he reappeared as an adept, saying: "I am ready for the next lesson."

Can you imagine what would happen to your consciousness if you meditated on those two words for several years? Even a few weeks of such contemplation could change your life![5]

Life in physical form is truly a school, and the wisdom teachings say it takes only three years to graduate—if one attends class daily, studies, and makes a concerted effort to understand and embody the spiritual principles.

Love of goodness without the will to learn casts the shadow called foolishness. Love of knowledge without the will to learn casts the shadow called instability. Love of truth without the will to learn casts the shadow called insensibility. Love of candour without the will to learn casts the shadow called rudeness. Love of daring without the will to learn casts the shadow called turbulence. Love of firmness without the will to learn casts the shadow called eccentricity.

The will to learn should be our driving motivation.

Does God speak? The four seasons hold on their course, and all things continue to live and grow. Yet, tell me, does God speak?

God is the sum-total of all energies—the one power and presence in the universe—that speaks to us through nature, through cosmic order and harmony, and through our own consciousness as we become more alive to the Spirit within and open our hearts and minds.

He who does not understand the Will of God can never be a man of the higher type. He who does not understand the inner law of self-control can never stand firm.

What is the Will of God? *A Course in Miracles* says that "God's Will for me is perfect happiness because there is no sin, and suffering is causeless. Joy is just, and pain is but the sign you have misunderstood yourself. Fear not the Will of God. But turn to it in confidence that it will set you free from all the consequences sin has wrought in feverish imagination."[6]

Yes! God's Will is perfect happiness and joy for all of us, which includes wholeness of mind and body, an all-sufficiency of supply, and ideal relationships as we journey through life together. The reference to the inner law of self-control by Confucius is the principle of ego-relinquishment—to place that insane thought-form under the authority of the spiritual Self. As we do this, the mortal part of us descends as Spirit rises. We then go forth as divine beings in a universe of love, free through the Will of God to enjoy the unfolding delights flowing through us moment by moment.

MEDITATE ON THESE IDEAS
FOR GREATER UNDERSTANDING

I choose to live with wisdom.

Beginning now I will think more and speak less, then follow with appropriate action.

I am inclusive, unconditional, reasonable, and flexible in all my relationships.

I consistently depend on the one Power, the one Cause—my Holy Self—for everything.

I follow the Golden Rule in every activity of my life.

I forgive myself and all others and close the door to the past. I no longer harbor feelings of guilt.

I listen, listen, listen—knowing that my guidance as a voice from God may come from even a stranger.

I am interested in others and treat them as I would want to be treated.

I love my Self and everyone else as my Self.

I work diligently to still my emotions, improve my mind, and to be true to who I am.

I am discerning.

I work for the greatest good of all.

I create beauty wherever I am.

I am totally dedicated to mastering the principles of life.

My will to learn is strong and powerful.

I am the wisdom of my Self in action. I am wise.

12

PAY FOR IT
AND TAKE WHAT
YOU WANT

Emerson asks, *"What will you have? quoth God; pay for it and take it."*[1]

What will you have? With love, forgiveness, and wisdom we have moved into an infinite realm of positive feasibility where anything conceivable is ready to come into form and experience. The kingdom of heaven has been found and the storehouse is jammed with delightful things, situations, episodes, circumstances—all tagged with our particular name.

We live and move and have our being in an energy field of wholeness, abundance, beauty, luxury, right livelihood, success, ideal relationships—you name it. And the "cashier" is standing there smiling, and saying, "Determine what will give you the greatest fulfillment at this moment in time, pay for it, and take it."

Are you out of a job? Pay for one and let it come looking for you. A health challenge? Pay for a healing and accept it. A shortage of money? Pay for what you need and watch the dollars come in. Want a meaningful relationship? Pay in advance and you'll find arms open wide to meet and greet you. The same principle applies even to houses, automobiles, new furnishings, and other "things."

How do we pay? By being consciously aware that whatever it is we seek is part of the reality of our Self, and by focusing that awareness on Self until the manifestation is complete.

When we focus our attention on our Self AS that which we are seeking, the Self is recognizing through our awareness that It IS that. And it is through our conscious one-pointed focus that the energy of Self is released into the phenomenal world to appear, manifest, express AS the job, the wholeness, the money, the relationship, the whatever.

We pay (offer as remuneration, compensation) with our thoughts and feelings focused on our spiritual Reality AS any- and everything we desire in life. And our thought (ideal) becomes Its thought—Its knowingness of Itself—and it is on this track-of-the-payment that the knowingness, as energy, becomes the thing, the experience.

Of course our Self knows all that there is to know about Itself. That is Knowingness in the absolute. But it is only when Self experiences what It is through our awareness that the manifestation takes place. Our Essential Being can only experience in the relative world what *we* know about Its attributes and qualities. And one doesn't have to be a metaphysician to participate in this creative process.

Look at the people who have been healed, supported, and protected through "faith." They fixed their minds on a higher power, and this believing in without wavering formed a parallel thought of knowledge just like the rails on a railroad track. And the train came forth to deliver. It never fails unless we throw the switch and cause a derailment.

I remember a man we once met—a true Superbeing. He said, "There's no excuse not to be well, rich, successful, and loved." Perhaps the only excuse is that we are not willing to pay in advance, even though Buddha, Confucius, Jesus, and other saints and saviors have said, "Give and you shall receive." And the reason we're not willing is because we have other priorities—or we're just plain lazy, not really caring enough to maximize our opportunities on this plane of life.

The best way that I've found to pay/give is through contemplative meditation, focusing on the quality of Self that I wish to have in a three-dimensional experience. If it's to write a particular book, I focus on Self as being that book—the nature, purpose, words—and on that beam of awareness, the energy of Self AS the qualities of the book streams forth into my consciousness. I've given, and received, and then it's up to me to do what I will with the gift.

I woke up one morning feeling joyless and a bit out of sorts. That's unusual for me, so before I got out of bed I focused on the quality of joy that my Self constantly lives with. I didn't affirm over and over that "I am joy!" Rather, I talked to my Self. I looked within at the Me of me and said, "YOU are the eternal energy of joy. YOU are never sad, sorrowful, unhappy— YOU don't even know what that means. YOU are always inspired and beside Yourself with rapturous delight."

Then I silently contemplated this truth. This action enabled Self to experience Itself as joy through my conscious awareness, which quickly bounced me out of bed with a song. Well, almost. At least there was one in my heart.

I should mention that just a momentary blink at Self won't make the connection. We have to be willing to spend hours a day if necessary in loving, joyful contemplation of Self AS the money, the wholeness of body, the right relationship, the true-place job. This relaxed but intense focus enables Self to see through our awareness, and what It sees, It experiences through us, as us.

Now let's look at this from another perspective.

YOU MUST HAVE UNLIMITED HEALTH, WEALTH, AND HAPPINESS

In my book *Angel Energy* I quote from Ageless Wisdom: "Within this divine, incorporeal, and eternal sphere (the archetypal plane) are included all that is, has been, or ever will be. Within the Kosmic Intellect all things spiritual or material exist as archetypes, or divine thought-forms."[2]

These archetypes, which I call angels in *The Angels Within Us* and *Angel Energy*, are extensions of our essential Self, much like shining rays from the sun. They represent particular energy vibrations, and when freed of ego control they become the manifesting agents of Spirit to bring our lives up to the divine standard. (See the Appendix for further information on these Living Energies.)

I also point out that "The angels in unity represent an infinite treasure house that exists right now within our energy fields."[3] They are a Unified Field— clusters of living intelligence and power in an interconnecting mass of energy existing just beyond the conscious level of mind. And while it is important that we deal with each angel separately to remove the ego projections, it is also necessary to work with them as a body of principle—the full force of *we-can-do-anything* power.

Jesus said, "You, therefore, must be perfect, as

your heavenly Father is perfect" (Matt. 5:48). As I said in *Angel Energy*, "This 'must be perfect' does not imply that it is a requirement; it means that it is a *certainty*."[4] Accordingly, when we know our Self, we know that we *must* have a perfect body, unlimited money supply, total victory, complete fulfillment, wonderfully loving relationships, and everything else that is good, true, and beautiful in life—*because it is a certainty and not just a possibility*. And when we impress a *certainty*, an *absolute Truth*, on the Unified Field of our causal powers with great feeling, they have no option but to express that certainty in visible form and experience.

How to work with the Unified Field. The Unified Field represents *potential* energy, which is changed to *kinetic* energy when activated by our thoughts and feelings. "Kinetic" comes from Greek and means *to move*. When the field is impressed by consciousness it moves into positive agitation. The energies of wholeness, supply, and success, for example, awake through our conscious awareness and move into action as law. Now they have no choice but to express, for that is the will and purpose of the Self, and what appears is wellness, wealth, and achievement in the degree of our understanding and acceptance.

Applying a law of physics to our spiritual metaphysical work, we remember that action of every force is accompanied by an equal reaction in the opposite direction. This means that an *inner* thrust of mind on the Unified Field results in an *outer* radiation as the potential energy is changed to kinetic, which becomes heat energy to manifest as form and experience. "Heat" in this case relates to fervency, intensity, eagerness to become that which can be observed and known.

Another law of physics also applies. When there is friction, the force needed to overcome it is proportional to the force causing the friction. For example, on the physical plane when the weight of something being pulled across the floor is doubled, the force necessary to pull it is doubled. The same principle applies in the manifestation process. If there is friction in consciousness (anger, fear, guilt, futility, etc.) there must be a proportional effort to overcome it. Yet still another law tells us that too much pressure decreases the flow of energy; it becomes resistant to the pressure. So the secret is to work with dedication and purpose—in proportion to the friction—while at the same time being relaxed and serene in mind and emotions and doing everything with ease and a sense of effortlessness. As a wise one once told me, "All spiritual work must be done with a feather duster."

Remember that whatever you desire, it is already a CERTAINTY in the Truth of Self. Therefore the fulfillment can be seen as an actuality, fact, reality in the phenomenal world—and this transition from something to come to what IS greatly influences the Unified Field. Here are a few starting points.

I MUST have a perfect body—vital, energetic, whole, for I am the principle of perfection, the law of wellness in action. I MUST be healthy. I MUST be whole.

I MUST have unlimited money supply right now, for that is the Truth of my Self—the fullness of universal wealth individualized. I MUST be rich.

I MUST be a world-class (artist, actor, musician, speaker, writer, manager, etc.) because my Master Self could not be anything else.

I MUST (fill in the blank):

_____

_____

_____

As soon as the conscious mind can comprehend this meaning of "must" without trying to think about it logically—understanding that it is already a done deal and not an aching hole in the heart to be filled, our truth is ready for placement in the creative stream. To do that we should remember that our objective consciousness, our thinking mind, must go into the Unified Field. This calls for the use of the imagination, and unless done properly, the manifestation will be delayed.

Now there are "seers" and "feelers." The seers can, through the mind's eye, "see" abstract form, light, color, etc., while the feelers cannot. They, in turn, must *feel* their way into the Unified Field, like someone with their eyes closed and arms outstretched slowly making their way through a crowded room.

If you are a feeler, *feel* the intensity of the environment, the high vibration, the love being radiated to you. Whichever you are, seer or feeler (or both), the key is to consciously enter, with purpose of mind, the field of living energies—the entrance-door being the heart center.

We move through the door consciously and see-feel the archetypes within taking notice. We let our conscious mind expand to encompass the entire Unified Field—all twenty-two power centers. We are now in touch with the creative forces of the universe. At this point look up to the apex of your energy field, to the gaze of the Holy Self, and dwell momentarily on the *Certainty Principle* relating to your intention.

Hear your Holiness say, "You MUST be ..." (whole, rich, successful) and get that truth fixed in your conscious mind. Then slowly drop your conscious awareness back into the Unified Field, and with feelings of love and joy silently speak your truth: "I MUST be ..." (whatever your desires are). And keep doing it until you feel a response, an acknowledgment, a vibratory confirmation. You might also intersperse images (mental pictures) of what your desire means to you.

How long and often do you do this? For as long as it takes to achieve positive and permanent results. Keep at it morning and night, every single day, until the creative activity is in full bloom.

During the process, keep your mind in the highest vibration possible. If a malady flags your attention, refuse to acknowledge it as having any reality. Look UP to the Master Self and say, "I MUST be whole and well because I AM"—and *live* with the idea of wholeness moment by moment.

Same thing for thoughts of scarcity or failure. Look UP from the lie and bathe in the MUST-be-rich, MUST-be-successful feelings. By doing this you are reinforcing the positive vibration of consciousness, the energy that you take into the Unified Field during those twice-a-day expeditions.

And remember that the angels are watching and listening all the time, and when they see that you are doing your best to break the lie of ego, they know you're serious—that your mind is made up—and that brings forth such a positive agitation that it can be felt across the far reaches of the universe.

When Jan had her heart attack and died on the EMS gurney—the paramedic looking at me and saying,

"We've lost her"—I remember a sense of detachment coming over me.

There's no use worrying about anything, everything's just fine.

In my mind she was whole, complete and radiantly healthy—impossible for anything to be wrong with her body. This was the MUST principle at work—a certainty registering in my consciousness—and this truth stayed with me all the time she was on the other side. The emotional roller coaster didn't begin until she returned to the body and we were racing to get her on the Airlife helicopter. That's when "logical mind" kicked in and I was scared silly that she wouldn't make it.

This happens to all of us. In the midst of the greatest crisis we can somehow separate ourselves from the mental-emotional energies and move up to a higher frequency. But the key is staying there throughout the emergency situation and being a channel for the healing and harmonizing light. That was tough for me. Weaving in and out of traffic while driving over a hundred miles per hour on the expressway I went through the peaks and valleys . . . *she's fine, no she's not . . . she's going to be all right, no she's dead.*

I know now that the more we practice the idea of MUST BE as the truth of Self, and thus as our truth, the longer we can remain in higher consciousness. It is also important—and this is the reason I'm referring to Jan's experience—that we use the MUST principle in every encounter we have with another person. Every time we "witness for truth" the must-be-perfection of someone else, we reinforce it for ourselves.

At least I did it to some extent. Jan gave me the opportunity to tell my story in her book, and here's an excerpt relating to that wild drive into San Antonio.

"Fortunately a horn honking in displeasure at my cutting in too close helped me to refocus, and as I took the exit ramp off the freeway, my mind cleared. A feeling of peace came over me, and I saw Jan's smiling face, the large, dark, shimmering eyes, and I knew it wasn't her time to go."[5]

My mind had shifted back into the Certainty mode, but we shouldn't need horns to refocus. Let's live with the MUST principle each and every day—for ourselves and others. Our effectiveness in serving on this particular plane of existence depends on it.

A MEDITATION

My Self is the wholeness and perfection of God. When I know this about my Self, I must be in radiant health. I know. When I know it about others, the reality behind the shadow is revealed. I see everyone as MUST BE WHOLE.

My Self is the abundance of the universe individu-

alized. *When I know this about my Self, I must be richly endowed. I know. When I see it in others, the energy of scarcity is transformed. I see everyone as MUST BE RICH.*

My Self is the essence, quality, and principle of all loving relationships. When I know this about my Self, all of my relationships must be divine and fulfilling. I know. When I witness for others, harmony is restored. I see everyone in a MUST-BE-FULFILLING relationship.

My Self is total triumph and achievement. When I know this about my Self, I must live in the continuing victory of true-place success. I know. When I see this in others, the energy of failure is transmuted. I see everyone as MUST BE SUCCESSFUL.

I keep my mind on the one Holy Self. I must be perfect. We are perfect.

13

SCIENTIFIC
PRAYER

Everything that is good, true, and beautiful in life is created out of the Mind and energy of our Divine Consciousness. This radiating activity of our essential Self is the eternally shining Sun. It is in constant operation, the energy forever being in perpetual motion to bring the Divine Plan of the Self into manifestation. When it flows through a conscious awareness of Itself, the power becomes what philosophers have called "the Divine Influence" in individual lives. Mystics refer to it as Grace—the goodwill of God in loving expression.

This is the "automatic mode" of living where our

primary function is to be consciously aware of the Presence within. The "manual mode" is when we deliberately focus on the form and deal strictly with the effects of this world. (When we worked with the Unified Field in the previous chapter we were conditioning consciousness for the automatic mode.) In manual we're using our minds to impress formulated thoughts of more money in the bank, more health in the body, etc., on the energy as though molding soft clay. Here we are working with the concept of impression-expression, or desire-oriented cause and effect. This is one form of applied metaphysics, and abundance, wholeness, and success can be the result of consciously impacting the law in this way.

Insufficiency, illness, and failure are also activities of the law as unconscious creations are impressed upon the energy through a negative mental atmosphere. Whether conscious or unconscious, whatever is impressed *on* the energy is expressed *by* the energy.

The problem with the manual mode is that we tend to dictate (outline) what will make us truly happy in life and we may not know. Our vision may be so clouded that we choose and accept far less than the true bliss that is God's will for us. We see and feel something that hurts—whether in our bodies, bank accounts, relationships, or jobs—and we try to relieve the pain. Our lives then become a course in pain management rather than a course of action in living joyfully with our inheritance.

I have had many opportunities to learn that the Way of Spirit is a higher path than the way of John Price. I've developed "mind models" to impress on the energy what I wanted expressed and have pounded the clay day after day. In one particular instance I got the message that I wasn't going to be satisfied with the outcome. Why? Because I was impressing mixed signals relating to personal desires. On top of that, I not only had decreed the end result in terms of material fulfillment, but I also set up the ways it was to be achieved.

I was reminded that personality does not have the wisdom, vision, or understanding to demonstrate anything but where it is in consciousness. Oh yes, we can impact the law and mold some clay, and for a time things may look better. But sooner or later our consciousness, unless changed, is going to bring everything back to its original shape.

Energy as creative power radiates from our Divine Consciousness, and moves through our mental and emotional system and out into the phenomenal world. The objective: to implement the Divine Plan of love, joy, and peace in our lives—the true desires of the heart. If the radiation picks up impressions with our I-want-to-make-something-happen treatment (which always includes our dominant beliefs), the experiences and situations created will be less than the divine standard.

We may perceive an improvement in our body and affairs, but after a time the same old problem will be calling for our attention. What the law has actually done is to demonstrate to us where we are in our understanding of Truth. (Most of us don't know what we really believe about life, God, and Self.)

This is not a condemnation of spiritual treatments. It is simply a suggestion that instead of trying to force the law to do our bidding, we use our treatments to practice the Presence of our Self.

As we provide a channel of Self-awareness for the energy, we move above the law and into a higher frequency. The energy, now operating as Grace—as the Divine Influence—will use that frequency to manifest forms and experiences that more closely mirror the Divine Intention. And the effect doesn't wear off in a matter of weeks and months.

I feel that many of us are afraid that if we don't take a conscious mind action to make something happen, the problem will just fester and grow. Maybe that's because we don't totally trust Spirit to act quickly in the most propitious way. We think we can do it faster and get the job done more to our liking. But we'll know better once we etch eight particular points deeply in consciousness. We'll get to those in a moment, but first a story.

In October of 1995 Jan and I conducted an Angel Mystery School in Cozumel, Mexico. One evening we left the hotel and took a cab into town and found a delightful French restaurant, spending several hours enjoying the different courses and fine wine. When we finally got back to the hotel there was a warning posted on the door. Hurricane Roxanne was scheduled to hit the island of Cozumel head-on the next day.

There's no sense worrying about anything, everything's just fine.

We've never had a Mystery School end with such a bang. The next morning our entire group went into prayerful meditation, each one of us working to move into a higher frequency in consciousness. And while we may not have been able to climb the ladder high enough for the maximum effect of Divine Influence, it did turn out to be a fun adventure.

By 2:30 that afternoon we and all the other hotel guests were in a "safe" room downstairs, awaiting Roxanne. And she came in with the fury of a nasty lady—blowing out windows, uprooting a few trees, and knocking out all power. A generator kept the lights on where we were—no air conditioning but everyone kept cool, played games and read books, told tall tales and giggled a lot. We were actually having fun during a "crisis." And I like to think that the energy of our group had a calming effect on most of the other people in the hotel and helped them to make the best of the situation.

THE PROGRAM OF THE 8 TO BECOME A CHANNEL FOR THE DIVINE INFLUENCE

Sometimes a particular ceremony is necessary to make a firm and lasting impression in mind and heart, especially one that combines the spoken word with physical movement. We will work with such an exercise in a moment, but first let's ponder these ideas, some of which have been previously discussed, others presented for the first time.

1. I have given up all resentment. I have forgiven all, and I am forgiven. I meditate on this for greater understanding.

2. I recognize my true worth and do not wish to be something other than what I am. God is not complete without me, which means that who I am is the most important part of the universe at the point where I am. I meditate deeply on this for greater understanding.

3. I have everything now because I have been given the Kingdom of Energies, and I give up the belief that there is anything missing in my life. The energy of everything I could possibly need or desire is right

here in my auric field right now. My Storehouse is full. The Power to be fulfilled in every area of my life is within me, ready to come forth into perfect form and manifestation. I meditate deeply on this for greater understanding.

4. I depend on the spirit–I AM within to bring this HAVE into visible expression; I cannot do it myself. My true nature knows what I need and will easily and lovingly provide for everything through my conscious awareness that It is doing so. I am now consciously aware of the activity of Truth, and regardless of appearances, I trust the Master within to take care of everything.

5. I make no judgments or come to any conclusions on anything that is mine to do. I decide for nothing except the spirit of God within and leave the entire decision-making process to the One Who Knows. My Holiness, in turn, makes up my mind for me quickly, easily, and firmly at the appropriate moment—and I am always pleased with my course of action. I begin each day by asking my Holy Self to make all decisions for me, as me.

6. I was created out of pure Love, and I eternally remain a creation of pure Love. Love is all there is. It is all that I can give, all that I can receive. As I recognize and understand this, my entire energy field is lifted to a higher frequency.

7. I know that when I *KNOW* my Self, I will never have another worry or concern in life. I

strengthen this knowingness now through contemplative meditation on the All that Self is.

8. I accept all that I AM, and all that I HAVE. I accept the magnificence of my Self, the completeness of my Self. I accept the fullness of my Self-expression, the total experience of having everything in the invisible *and* the visible. I meditate deeply on this for greater understanding.

LET US WALK THE 8

The old masters believed 8 was a sacred number that could be used in reawakening ourselves to the Holy One within. As a daily exercise to supplement the meditations and release the Divine Influence, see with your mind's eye a large figure 8 on the floor in front of you. (You may want to lay one out with tape or string.)

Go to the center of the 8 where the two circles meet, close your eyes and move into the Light within. Feel the Presence and acknowledge that you are now standing in your God Self.

Now follow the higher circle of the 8, taking two steps and stopping at the lower right point. At this first station of the 8, say, *I forgive and I am forgiven.*

Following the curve of the circle, take two steps and pause at the upper right. At this second station, say, *I am the Worthiness of God as me.*

Continue over to the upper left part of the circle,

the third station, and say, *I have everything now; nothing is missing in my life.*

Proceed to the fourth station at the lower left point of the upper circle. Pause, and say, *I am aware of my Holy Self, and through this awareness all things good are made manifest.*

Walk past the center point of the circles to the upper right of the lower circle. Pause at this fifth station and say, *Every decision I make has already been made by my Holy Self.*

At the sixth station, the lower right of the bottom circle, pause and say, *I am a creation of love, and I love my Holy Self with all of my being.*

At the seventh station, the lower left of the bottom circle, say, *I know my Self, and through this knowingness I am totally fulfilled.*

Finally, moving to the upper left point of the lower circle, pause at this eighth station and say, *I accept all that I AM and HAVE, and allow myself the experience of heaven on earth.*

I recommend that you commit each statement of the stations to memory, then slowly walk the 8 twice a day as a high ceremony of love, devotion, and reawakening to joy.

Walking the 8 to Reawakening

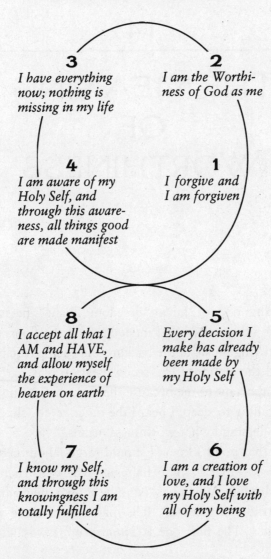

3
I have everything now; nothing is missing in my life

2
I am the Worthiness of God as me

4
I am aware of my Holy Self, and through this awareness, all things good are made manifest

1
I forgive and I am forgiven

8
I accept all that I AM and HAVE, and allow myself the experience of heaven on earth

5
Every decision I make has already been made by my Holy Self

7
I know my Self, and through this knowingness I am totally fulfilled

6
I am a creation of love, and I love my Holy Self with all of my being

14

THE MEANING OF WORTHINESS

During one of Jan's "Freedom Flight" personal growth workshops I made an 8 on the floor, and with stirring music in the background each participant walked the stations. The second station was particularly important to me because the night before, just as I was falling to sleep, I heard the inner voice ask, "Do you understand what worthiness means?"

At that point I knew I should forget about getting any sleep—that's what happens when instructions come through. When I asked to be shown the meaning of worthiness, I heard, "It is made up of three vital attributes. The first one is *innocence*." I was left to ponder the added dimensions of that word and to look at the energy behind the word.

"Innocence" means *guiltlessness, blamelessness*. It is *simplicity*. How does this relate to worthiness? If we feel guilty about something, and continue to blame ourselves, it's going to be difficult to recognize our true worth. Guilt and worthiness just don't mix. And what about simplicity? If that's one of our characteristics it means that we are honest, open, natural, and free of the complex pomposity of an ego-dominated personality. When life becomes uncomplicated, consciousness is less fractured—which means that we can then focus on what's really meaningful in life. And the feelings of self-worth move beyond ego control. Using simplicity as an example, let me show you how spirit works to solve a problem.

Jan and I had been meditating for guidance in a particular situation concerning the Quartus Foundation, the organization that we founded in 1981 to serve as the research and communications base for our activities. We needed to make some decisions and couldn't get a clear picture of what to do.

There's no sense worrying about anything, everything's just fine.

When the specific direction didn't come immediately we released the "need" to spirit. A couple of days later—on a Sunday afternoon—Jan asked me to go with her to a near-death seminar in San Antonio. As we listened to the experiences of others in their trip to the other side, the facilitator asked a man in the front row the most important thing he had learned from his visit to that other dimension. He said without hesitation, *"Keep it simple."*

As he spoke those words, an electric shock hit me and I knew I had the answer to my meditative request. *Keep it simple!* He went on to say that his instruction from the heavenly realm was to enjoy the simplicity of life by keeping things uncomplicated—just the opposite of what I was trying to do with Quartus. We followed the guidance and things turned out beautifully.

An hour later on that night of instruction, the next aspect came through. The inner voice said, "The second attribute of worthiness is *humility*." And again I was given the opportunity to ponder the word in its fullness.

Many of us may equate humility with weakness, whereas just the opposite is true. Just look at the antonyms of humility: pride, arrogance, rudeness, vanity, pretentiousness, pomposity, and boastfulness. A person known for these characteristics is indeed weak.

I was on a radio talk show broadcast from Rhode Island in 1995—the subject being angels. During the show the host asked me about conditioning consciousness for work with the angels within us, and I brought up the idea of worthiness. At one point she said, "Of all the true spiritual people I've met in this world over the past thirty years, one thing stands out: They were courteous. People who are innately positive about life are courteous, gracious, respectful, and show good manners." I agreed. They know their worthiness.

True humility means being open and receptive to new ideas. It is being unpretentious. It is the consciousness of consent, a willingness to be shown the higher path through a surrender of the lower personality. With humility our true worthiness begins to shine as the noonday sun. Without it a form of rigidity may set in, which becomes another experience to work through.

Maybe we get hooked on a particular book or teacher and become closed-minded spiritual snobs. Jan and I ran into a few such people one evening when someone asked us to speak at a small gathering. *Their* teacher possessed the highest truth and we didn't, and we were given a rather rude reception. We laughed about it later and remembered our narrow-minded times when only the author of the current book we were reading was considered right and true.

Or perhaps we get testy because we begin to see the unlimited possibilities of life, and with that new vision we lose patience with anyone who doesn't share our perception. I certainly turned off a lot of people in my Houston advertising agency by constantly spouting metaphysical clichés and being peeved at those who didn't "get it." Humility? Hardly.

Sometimes a touch of spiritual reality will make us want to escape from life, and we start to resent anyone who might suggest that we get with the program—that life is supposed to be run *with*, not away *from*. This hasn't been our experience but we've known others who wanted liberty more than life.

This brings up the job-money issue. With some teachings offering a license to find bliss by doing nothing, resentment grows toward those who have decided to stay in the world, contribute something, and enjoy the fruits of their labors—for the fun of it. With humility in mind and heart, we stop judging others and ourselves—and that's when true freedom begins.

Still later on that night of worthiness instructions, the third part of the message came through. The voice said, "The third attribute of worthiness is *reverence*." And in my contemplation I asked for what? And the answer was, "For life, and all that is involved in it."

Reverence means deep respect, regard, honor, devotion—to revere our livingness, to cherish the opportunity we have in this incarnation to open our hearts, stretch our minds, and reawaken to all the joys that life has to offer. How many of us practice reverence in our homes—with our children, our spouses; in our work—with our employers, our coworkers; on the thoroughfare of life—with the people we encounter? Reverence is a state of mind, and as we acquire it, our self-worth blossoms as a flower.

I know that since Jan's near-death experience, we both have a deeper reverence for life—and for each other. I'd like to quote another passage from her book here. She says,

> I think death is most interesting because it makes you think a lot about life. . . . I want to live life fully, and I don't know how long I've got. No one gave me a schedule or timetable.
>
> I know John wants to make every moment count. He's rarely planned anything special for his birthday, but that particular February celebration, six weeks after my hospital stay, was quite different. He arranged for a suite at a fine hotel in San Antonio—one offering "luxury and intimacy"—made reservations at a continental restaurant, and called two other couples—close friends—to join us for dinner. Later that night, on *his* birthday, he gave me a gift—a beautiful red silk robe and nightgown. And as he wrote about it later,

We let the air be charged with the lovely fragrance of delightful romance. The next day we saw San Antonio in a completely different way. It was no longer an old, crowded city—it was a jewel, a gem of beauty and charm, filled with wonderful, happy people expressing life and love. We shopped as tourists, laughed with the vendors, skipped along the River Walk waving at the smiling faces in the boats, smelled the gorgeous flowers, listened to the music, ate like starving kids, and had a magnificent time.

We were learning to play.[1]

I believe that when we live with joyful reverence—for the fun of it—our worthiness soars because we have touched the true meaning of life. Through innocence, humility, and reverence we will begin to remember our worthiness as a creation of God, as a divine individual. We are worthy of wholeness and radiant health. We are worthy of lavish abundance. We are worthy of loving, lasting relationships. We are worthy of grand success—of victory and triumph over every trial and tribulation. After all, each one of us is a vital piece of the Cosmic Puzzle.

A MEDITATION

I was created by God and eternally live in God, with God, as the spirit of God. The fullness of the Godhead dwells in me and expresses through me as every good and perfect thing. I am a channel for positive change in this world.

I recognize my value as an individual being living on earth at this time. As the very worthiness of God, I am part of the Grand Plan of continuing creation, and my contribution to this world is vitally important in the divine scheme of things.

Poised, powerful, and peaceful, I do my part with love and joy. I am guiltless, open and receptive to right action, and devoted to my purpose in life. Everything I do is meaningful and worthwhile. I am deserving because I know who I am.

15

ONE GOD IS
ENOUGH

I have heard people say that they learned the truth of
health and wholeness by being sick, the reality of
abundance by suffering lack, the beauty of harmonious relationships by witnessing firsthand the ugliness
of discord. Such educational experiences may be fine
for some, but they remind me of the old joke about the
person who hit himself on the head with a hammer so
it would feel good when he stopped.

Many of us do that—worship the hammer god as
our way of seeking the good life. No wonder the wise
ones shake their heads and wonder why we can't
accept the fact that the only problems we have are

those of our own creation. They know this is a strictly loving universe with joy as its song—that everything in life is meant to be positive, and that if God didn't cause it, it isn't so.

I think it's a wonderful thing to know that our challenges are self-created. With no one to blame we can stop fearing what's "out there" and start taking charge of our lives. Remember that we live in a frequency world, and we experience the frequency that we are registering. Those below the 50 percent level are exposed to the turmoil of the collective ego, and the greater the descent, the greater the savagery. From the midpoint up, the ascent takes us more and more out of the illusion and closer to reality.

Many of us bob up and down on the scale. That's when negative experiences can creep in—at a time and point when we're vulnerable. But instead of rising in consciousness above the problem we harness all of our creative energy to focus on it and give it more power over us. Why? The same reason the media concentrates on the bad and the ugly: It's *unnatural*.

Anything abnormal in life fascinates us, whether in the body, bank account, or in relationships. And what we focus our attention on grows—the malady intensifies, the lack produces more of its kind, and the discord gets harsher—because energy follows thought.

When we can remember that the only problems we

have are those we have entertained in our house of consciousness, we'll start being discerning. Just because Mr. Ill, Mrs. Limitation, or Ms. Disharmony knocks on the door doesn't mean we have to invite them in. Sometimes all it takes is, "Please leave. You are not welcome in this house."

Why can't we accept the fact that positive living is the natural way of life? For one thing, orthodox religion has told us something different, which means that we may have to do some deprogramming on ourselves. We have to move past the false teachings that tell us we're a race of damned and doomed cosmic misfits who played with a garden snake, then learned a thousand years later that the only antidote, the only salvation, was a vicarious blood sacrifice. That notion didn't come from Jesus.

A Course in Miracles says that

> If the crucifixion is seen from an upside-down point of view, it does appear as if God permitted and even encouraged one of His Sons to suffer because he was good. This particular unfortunate interpretation, which arose out of projection, has led many people to be bitterly afraid of God.... Persecution frequently results in an attempt to "justify" the

terrible misperception that God Himself perse-
cuted His Own Son on behalf of salvation. The
very words are meaningless. . . . I was not
"punished" because you were bad. The wholly
benign lesson the Atonement teaches is lost if it
is tainted with this kind of distortion in any
form.[1]

Another reason for our unacceptance of total good
is that unpleasant experiences with people in and
out of the family unit may have conditioned us to
expect something less than positive in life. This is why
closing the door to the past and throwing away the
key is crucial, to be followed by a complete change
of attitude about life and living. The next time a
problem arises, ask yourself: What is my Reality
seeing and saying? The answers will quickly tell you
that all is perfect *now*—not to come in the future,
but now.

My dog Maggi and I were walking through the
fields early one morning at first light. We heard a
rustling in some high brush and she sprang in to check
it out, then slowly backed away—in my direction—
nose to nose with a large skunk.

There's no sense worrying about anything, every-
thing's just fine.

I froze, then tried to see what was happening from

a high vision. *Watch life enjoying itself!* Maggi and the skunk began playing, jumping around and smelling each other while I stood motionless, eyes wide, not more than a few feet away. After a few minutes the skunk seemed to say, "For a dog you're okay, now I've got to be going," and walked rapidly back into the darkness of the foliage.

Yes, it *is* a kindhearted and compassionate universe.

Just recently Jan and I got into our car at a busy shopping center. I started the engine, checked my rearview mirror, put the gear into reverse and pressed on the accelerator. Nothing happened. I shifted back into park, then into reverse again, and as I applied the gas it was as though some mighty force was holding the car. "What's going on?" I asked. *Check your blind spot!* I adjusted the side mirror and saw a gold Mercedes, its front end behind my left rear bumper. The driver was waiting for another car to exit a parking space. As soon as the Mercedes pulled on down, the backward motion of my car worked perfectly.

Jan was watching the whole thing, and as we eased out, she said, "That's another angel story. Helping hands held you back until the way was clear."

The full-of-goodwill universe includes those Living Energies within us who work for the good of all.

Why do we blame God for the traps on the path? Because we believe, rightly, that God's will is the only power, that God's authority is absolute, and God's law is the only cause. But what does God will, authorize, and cause? Certainly not sickness, scarcity, or suffering. *We just don't have a mean old God.* The only God there is is the law, the principle, the author, the revealer of wholeness, abundance, and happiness.

Once we accept this truth we may look to someone else (another god) to blame for our woes—husband, wife, son, daughter, boss, and so on. Then one day it dawns on us that he-she is only playing back to us what we're projecting, and we come face to face with the source of the trouble—the one in the mirror.

We understand now, but that doesn't keep us from continuing to look for another god to hold responsible. I knew an allergy sufferer who was told his sneezing must be the result of low self-worth. He immediately began to look for reasons his self-esteem had diminished. Probably began as a child, he thought, when his father told him he couldn't do anything right. Becomes angry at father. Then he remembered an action he had taken on the job, which his employer frowned upon. Must be that. Becomes resentful toward employer.

He was focusing on the problem, not the healing correction in consciousness, and his mind zeroed in on the ideas of uselessness, fruitlessness, and futility as his new gods.

Going all the way back to Sanskrit we find that the root word of god is "invoked one." *Invoke* means "to call forth, to summon." So in this context, god is whatever we call forth and give power to. And that's what some of us are doing—summoning the god of sickness to teach us wholeness, the god of scarcity to show us the truth of abundance, the god of unemployment to find our true place. That's like inviting Dracula to teach a course on the positive benefits of sunshine.

What we must do is deal only with *The* God, the Almighty, the Father-Mother Supreme Being, our Creator Who is expressed as the True Self of everyone. Let's put our attention on *The God Within*—that field of infinite, positive, ready-for-immediate-expression possibilities. This is not something separate from us; it is *What* we are. And in this energy field there are no problems because its nature—*our* nature—is perfect.

As the very Kingdom of God we are never unemployed, uncreative, uninspired, unfulfilled, or unable to do what we came to accomplish on this plane. The next time we feel less than we are, let's remind ourselves (1) Our Holy Self does not feel anger, fear, guilt, insecurity, confusion, rejection, or whatever the negative emotion may be, (2) I am my Holy Self, and therefore (3) I cannot experience that emotion.

We are not effect, we are Cause, and as Cause we can stop fooling around with false gods—which means we don't have to experience the darkness to understand the light.

A MEDITATION

I shall not ask God for anything in prayer. Rather I will acknowledge God as having already manifested that which I seek.

That which I seek—whether health, prosperity, right relationships, right livelihood, creative expression, love, joy, peace, inspiration, or guidance—is already fully expressed within me. Therefore I have no unfulfilled desires, and to pray for these experiences of wholeness is to deny that they have already been satisfied, which becomes a prayer for unfulfillment. Today I cease praying for that which I do not want.

The fullness of the expression I am seeking is within me now, in my consciousness. It is the Kingdom of God, the Universal Wholeness, the Cosmic Treasury. I gently and purposely rise into that higher realm.

I am in my reality now. I am in Me. I am in True Consciousness where all my good has eternally existed, where God is fully manifest. I see, feel, know that anything I could possibly need or want is right here, where I am, right now.

This total and complete fulfillment in every area

and aspect of life exists in the invisible essence of my True Nature. I am aware of the particular good that I seek, and see it shining as a point of light, a divinely imaged impression, an imprinted thought-form blazing as a starburst in consciousness. This pulsating reality is now expanding, filling my awareness with its light.

With great feeling I express my thankfulness, and acknowledge that the good I have been seeking is what I AM. I have been looking for my Consciousness. I have been looking for Me. I have found Me. I now have everything.

The effortless task before me now is to simply open the door and release the splendor that I have imprisoned through unknowing. With my inner vision I see the door before me. It swings inward, not outward, so I do not have to push. I place my hand on the knob, turn it, and feel the movement of the opening door.

Simultaneously I feel the incredible rushing force, the awesome energy in motion as it finds an outlet through the wide open door. The love, intelligence, and power of I AM has gone before me to be in the outer world what it was in the inner. Consciousness has extended itself from thought to form.

I keep the door open by laughing with my Self over the idea that I thought something was missing in my life. I continue to release the dynamic energy of fulfillment by keeping my mind focused on the source of fulfillment within.

The bridge between the inner and outer is com-

plete, and the activity of God is the only power at work in my life.

I now prepare for the inevitable, inescapable, certain, and sure proof of this.

It is happening now. Praise God!

16

LIVING THE GOOD LIFE

What does "the good life" mean to you? While there will be a few common denominators, the answers from a thousand people would cover a broad spectrum, tailored to the individual's supposed needs, wants, and desires—and to the intuitive response to the Self's purpose in this lifetime.

I asked several people—not necessarily the type who would be reading this book—for an immediate top-of-mind definition of *the good life*. The response was interesting:

> *Having everything when I want it . . . I'm not the waiting type.*

Not having to worry about money.
To know I'll be secure later in life.
To feel good without concern for my body.
Good sex, more money, and running my own
show (business).
Retiring in the Caribbean with a neat woman and
plenty of money.
Being at peace and satisfied with everything
around me.
Contented, both financially and spiritually.
To have the right man in my life—to get married.
To have a fulfilling career that pays well.

How would you define the good life? We all want peace of mind, a sense of freedom to pursue what we consider our life's goals, a healthy body to carry us through our third-dimensional expedition, an all-sufficiency of dollars for financial independence, and right relations with those who are part of our experience. I have had all of the above at various periods in my life and still didn't feel that I was truly *living*. Something was missing, and it took several years to discover what it was.

THE MISSING INGREDIENT

It was eventually revealed to me from within that I could not live a life of true joy if I depended on the personality of John Price or anyone else to provide it. My physical, emotional, and mental systems simply did not have the drive, power, vision, or intelligence to put me in a state of bliss and keep me there—and neither did any other person in my world. It was only then that I got a hint of what "the good life" was really all about.

You see, there are two worlds out there—one created by the collective ego, the other by the universal Self, which individualizes as each one of us. If we try to manipulate and change the ego world to make us happy—or rely on others to help us do it—we'll spend the rest of our lives trying to repair a broken down old shack. However, if we move into the consciousness of our essential Self, what we see through our human eyes is replaced by what is seen in true vision. That's when we see what our Self wants to do—its purpose— and then life becomes truly an exciting adventure.

One way that's been helpful to me is to frequently remind myself that every activity of my life is being managed and governed "upstairs." In that Divine Consciousness overshadowing us is the embodiment of every right idea corresponding to every perfect form and experience in life. And these thoughts, approaches, paradigms, patterns, and optimal goals relating to the activities of health, wealth, relationships, creativity, and physical things are not static and passive. They are active and dynamic as highly charged beams of kinetic energy constantly in motion. Thus "production" is constantly being carried out in the Power Plant above—and that which is produced in Mind is always governed by Mind, which means that such things as failure, loss, delays, and frustration can never be a part of the manifest expression.

Again, this does not mean that we live a do-nothing life or give up all desires. Yes, the Master Self is the manager, governor, producer—but Divine Mind wants us to be of one accord with its purpose, and that's why we feel those intense yearnings to do, be, or have. It is through a *fearless* mind of similar intent—a consciousness of consenting vibration—that Self works. So as part of living the good life, determine what it is you want more than anything else in the world—the burning passion of your true heart's desire. Hold it close and never let it go. It's your inspiration, your purpose, your dream, which is how your higher nature wishes to express in this incarnation. It gets your attention through the energy of your hopes, wishes, and dreams.

Our realization of our Divine Consciousness AS everything good, true, and beautiful—including our life's purpose—puts us in alignment with the spiritual laws that bring forth the invisible "good life" into visibility. *Alignment* means to "line up." Take two boards and drill a hole in each one, then place one board on top of the other. Unless the holes match up, there is no opening from one side to the other and nothing can get through. But when they are aligned, there is a clear channel. Same thing with us. When we are aligned with our Spirit-Self, the energy, light, substance flows easily and powerfully into manifestation.

How do we get into alignment with the Master Mind and stay there? Consider these points:

1. Control the ego. How do we break the grip of the ego? That's what we've been doing in this book, but as we realize that *nothing is impossible* we may unconsciously slip back into its clutches. Let's watch our feelings of self-importance and not forget how dangerous a minefield arrogance, pride, and swagger can be. Also, a greater understanding that *all good things are possible* may depress us at first because such things are not happening in our lives. This could throw us into the victim role. Victim can be an interesting character to play. Posture: sagging shoulders. Facial expression: grim. Voice: whiny. Words from script with camera close up: "I don't deserve this; why can't good things happen to me?" Ego gets credit for fine direction. Whenever self-importance and depression weigh in, take control. Meditate on who and what you are and let the light dispel the shadows.

2. Break the connection with our identities as humans. As I wrote in *A Spiritual Philosophy for the New World*, "We do this by recognizing that on the human level we will never get out of the revolving door, and by acknowledging the greatest spiritual

secret in this world: '*I can of myself do nothing.*' This is not resignation; this is *power thinking.* As the Ageless Wisdom stated it, and later echoed by Paul, 'Have nothing and you possess everything.' This must be our creed if we are to gain our freedom and be all that we were created to be."[1] I go on to recommend the sixty-day nonhuman program where not a single prayer is uttered for any material form or experience. Rather, all spiritual work is done only for a greater awareness, understanding, and knowledge of your Master Self and a deeper recognition of the activity of that Self. I invite you to try the nonhuman program as outlined in that book for two months, supplemented with the following activities.

3. Continue daily meditation on the One Presence within, recognizing the fullness of every attribute, the infinite wholeness of Being—nothing missing—and understanding that what we are gazing at is our very own individual Consciousness. Ask yourself, "Would not this infinitely loving Mind know how to take care of any problem I might have? Could there be any question too difficult? Would not the solution and the answer already be there, simply waiting to be acknowledged?" The pulsation in your heart—the feeling of Truth—tells you that you are never alone, that your Holiness is constantly and continually going before you to straighten out every crooked place in life, remove every obstacle, and perform what we think of as miracles. This concurrence, this meeting of

minds in conscious agreement, permits the Divine Influence to impact the feeling nature with the Truth that God is in charge of our lives (not the ego) and there is nothing to fear.

4. Relax more and don't let the tensions build. Brush the spark off the sleeve before it burns a hole. Since the work is being done in higher consciousness, our role is simply to let go and let God—to trust the only Cause for joy—while holding to our vision, our dream, without fearing that it won't come to pass. This is *having faith*. Faith is the energy of that which is to become a visible experience. It is the energy of conviction leading to the total acceptance of the Law of Harmony. Without wavering from what we consider our purpose in life, we surrender every problem and concern, get lighter, and remember that fun is holy—as Jan was told on the other side. We keep our mind on the Presence, listen to the voice within for any action we are to take, honor our divinity by committing our life to Spirit, and watch as the divine expressions take place.

5. Love and enjoy that which Spirit creates and reveals. When our hopes, wishes, and dreams appear substantial in this world, let's not deny them by saying we're above materialism. We focus on Cause as the creator of our world, and through our Self-awareness the energies are "arrested" and the ideal things and experiences take on three-dimensional structure. Then we go forth to play in the fields of the harvest. We treasure the

beauty, comfort, wellness, affluence, victory—not as cause but as the fruits of the dynamic divine process.

6. Practice frequent joyful glances at the beloved Self within, expressing deep love for our Immortal Being. Remember the sixth step in "walking the 8" is to love our Self with all our mind and heart, which forms a magnetic attraction and draws us into the inner realm of our Divine Consciousness. There we begin to know our Self as never before (step seven), and through this knowing, the Truth of being is expressed in the heart center. And it is this Truth energy, this *feeling* of profound understanding, that reveals harmony, wholeness, abundance, and right relations. So love is the step that leads to knowing, which registers as Truth, which goes before us to dissolve the illusory world—and the ego with it.

7. See the Divine in everyone rather than the human. If we see less in others, we're seeing less in ourselves. Perhaps this is why I don't counsel people. I don't really see or agree with their "problems" regardless of what they say—and this isn't what they want to hear. I can be compassionate and understanding with what they are professing, but in my mind I see only their perfection. Interestingly, this attitude has produced healings without any conscious effort on my part. As I discovered this was happening, I began to dwell even more on overlooking the human in me. Sometimes it's easier to see perfection in others than in one's self.

8. Be one with nature and know we are seeing the One Presence and Power in glorious expression. Rise up above the illusory scene and with high vision see the beauty, wholeness, and harmlessness of the true natural world where everything is in balance and harmony. This state of consciousness will help tame the collective ego's effect on nature—the rampage in the form of destructive forces.

9. Listen to music that touches our heart and soul and brings our energy centers into a higher state of vibration. Here are some selections for the appropriate center: The crown chakra—*Greensleeves* (Traditional); the third-eye chakra—*Ave Maria, Op. 52 No. 6*, Schubert; the throat chakra—*Symphony No. 5, Allegro con brio*, Beethoven; the heart chakra—*Adagio* from *Symphony No. 2, Op. 27*, Rachmaninoff; the solar plexus chakra—*Laura's Theme* from *Doctor Zhivago*; the sacral chakra—*Sakura, Sakura* (Traditional); the root chakra—*Rite of Spring* (Stravinsky).

10. Be able to accept with great happiness that which we would consider totally unacceptable in life. This will enable us to embrace a new life so filled with joy and peace that we will think we've moved into another dimension—and we have.

The tenth point above was given to me during a period of ponderings about the direction my life was taking. I was holding to my dream but seemed to be in a period where everything was frozen, barren—

nothing was happening. It was as if all communications from the "outside" had been cut off, the still small voice within was *very* still, and I felt that I didn't have anything else to write about or share in workshops. Even the staff at the Quartus Foundation felt like Maytag repairmen—few phone calls or letters.

So in addition to my normal ways of getting back into alignment (I wanted answers fast), I stormed the gates of the divine energy with a loud voice and demanded to know what was going on. The message came loud and clear: *"Until you can accept the unacceptable with great happiness, you cannot embrace the fuller life."*

Oh great. Now I had to decide what was unacceptable, and then find happiness by accepting what I didn't want. It didn't take long. I had filled three pages of a yellow pad with what I found unacceptable when Jan came in. I told her what I was doing and she joined me—throwing out ideas of what she found unacceptable and accepting them. We didn't care if we ever wrote another book, gave another workshop, sold any more books, or if Quartus closed its doors—and kept ranting and raving about letting everything go, including the passion of the dream. And suddenly we found ourselves giggling like little kids—and we felt freer than we had in years.

In the days and weeks that followed, wondrous things began to happen. Ideas for a book began to form in my mind, which was quickly followed by a call from my editor asking that I write a new spiritual book. It's the book you're reading now. Then Hay House, Inc., an international leader in publishing self-help and transformational books, agreed to buy all of my books formerly published by Quartus and reissue them with a major marketing effort. Jan's book *The Other Side of Death* was released to excellent reviews. I wrote a novel in six weeks—one of those flow-through writings from beginning to end, and I'm sure it will be published at the appropriate time. A West Coast book tour was set up for us with lectures, work-shops, media appearances, and bookstore signings in cities from Seattle to San Diego—and we loved every minute of it. The phones started ringing and the mail picked up at Quartus. And even the leaky roof on our house repaired itself without anything being done.

Do you see the real message of accepting the unac-ceptable? It's giving up fear of the future. It means to stop being afraid something won't happen and to live in the glorious *now*. If we dwell in concern over the tomorrows of life, we lose today and close the door on the good that is to appear at the right time and in the right way. In *The Superbeings* I wrote that when we care (worry) too much, we divert the power flow. How easy it is to forget.

What does "the good life" mean to you? You may not know until you turn your life over to Spirit—and then everything changes. Peace comes, the tension and stress leave, and you begin to live with ease. There's joy and fulfillment. Unconditional love seems to have taken over your consciousness and you attract right relationships into your life—and the ones from the past are harmonized. You feel good physically and emotionally, and the relaxed mind is sharper, more intuitive. Money is plentiful and there's no concern about future financial security. You are inspired to do that which is yours to do, and your creative endeavors meet only with success. Your entire personal world is in divine order and you live for the pure joy of it. This is living the good life, and the only goal in mind and heart now is to continue being an open channel for the activity of your Divine Consciousness.

A MEDITATION

God is fully manifest as my Consciousness. God is my individual being, my reality. All that God is, I AM. All that God has is mine. I am totally complete, whole.

Within my Divine Mind is the perfect idea of every thing I could possibly need, want, or desire in this world. Guidance and protection are there, speaking to me and overshadowing me at every moment. The spirit of fearlessness enfolds me. Ideal relationships are there along with true-place success, the perfect body, financial plenty, a home of great beauty, and every other form and experience that would contribute to blissful living. All that I could ever seek I have.

All that is within my Consciousness is eternally and easily being extended, expressed, and made manifest in the phenomenal world without any effort on my part. Forms of utter delight are continually being revealed. Experiences of great joy are constantly pouring through my Self-awareness to be lived by me in pleasure and jubilation.

I dedicate my life to the Spirit of God within me, my Holy Self, and keep my mind fixed on this loving Presence that I AM. I relax. I contemplate. I listen. I watch. The law of harmony is ruling my world. My life is wonderful.

17

THE BRIGHT LIGHT ON THE HORIZON

Earlier I mentioned fear of the future. I said, "If we dwell in concern over the tomorrows of life, we lose today . . ." Yet hardly a week goes by that I don't receive a letter expressing concern about what's on the horizon. I realize that at one time or another each one of us has thought about the world that is waiting for us around the corner, or a few years down the road, and how we will be affected individually. But if we're going to live joyfully in the Fourth Dimension, we'd better relax, see only a positive future, and ignore the Dweller's attempts to sway us with the promise of upcoming trials and tribulations. There are no such things unless we choose to *believe* there are.

At the end of one December, Jan and I were discussing what to let go of as we began the new year. She said, "I see that which must be left behind is 'the belief in' whatever I choose to let go of, for the 'belief in' is what causes 'the manifestation of.' So I let go of the belief that there is or can be any kind of limitation. I let go of the belief in delay, impediment, blockage of any kind. I let go of the belief that anyone is wrong, that anyone is without love and fulfillment. I let go of the belief in stress, tension, discord, illness, aging; that there is any lack of time or energy. I let go of the belief that I do not live in a perfect, harmonious, joyous, prosperous, loving world."

We—all of us—can live in a perfect world as we release all beliefs to the contrary. We let them go and move into a state of *knowing* by looking through the lens of spiritual consciousness. That has been the purpose of our journey in this book—to discover the real world within us and let it be expressed through us. And from that higher vision we see that we are living there now and we're clapping our hands with joy, for there is only peace, financial plenty, wholeness, harmony, understanding, wisdom, and right action—now and for the future.

Not only is a large segment of the population moving into this higher frequency and *living there*, but Reality itself is slowly but surely changing the dense energies of the physical world. When Jan was on the other side and looking back at this one, she saw the light growing, spreading, and knew with all her heart that this world is being lifted into a higher and finer vibration. In truth, the Dweller is reaching the stage of impotence.

In our spiritual consciousness we know now that it is God's will for us to live in perfect peace with overflowing joy and happiness. This means that all things good, true, and beautiful have already been given to us, which includes the answer to every question and the supply for every need we could possibly have. So we live in a consciousness of *HAVE*, and in this completeness we see each individual in this world—regardless of appearances—as possessing the fullness of the kingdom now.

"Individual" is defined by Webster as *not divisible, not separable.* Grasp that in its fullness. It means we are all a part of a united Soul-base that cannot be divided. Thus, I am a part of you and you are part of me and we are one eternally. This is why we must not see each other as poor, sick, unfulfilled, fearful, and burdened with guilt. That is impossible in spiritual vision and that is the vision we must hold. To see through the eyes of ego and behold someone else as less than perfect is to call forth into manifestation that which is not desired for us individually.

Our reality is God. We are nonphysical spiritual beings and nothing else exists. Abundance created us rich; Wholeness created us in an eternal state of well-being; Love created us loved and loving; Success created us as totally triumphant in every activity of life.

Denial of this truth produces needs where there were none. Knowledge of our sacred Self eliminates the needs, for the Self is the principle of fulfillment. What we observe within we become. And let's remember that joy and sadness cannot exist simultaneously. When we choose one, the other cannot be. We have chosen joy and left the other in the wake.

In 1984 I wrote "The World Healing Meditation" to be used at noon Greenwich time each December 31st beginning in 1986. Over 500 million people participated on that first World Healing Day, and with millions of people all over the world continuing to meditate on, think about, and speak these words for over a decade—not only at the end of the year but also regularly throughout each month—a bright light has emerged on the horizon. And through the concepts, meditations, and new understanding offered in this book, we have been steadily moving toward that light. To permanently secure our future in this radiance, let's pause for a moment and remind ourselves that . . .

In the beginning
In the beginning God
In the beginning God created the heaven and
*   earth.*
And God said Let there be light: and there was
*   light.*

Now is the time of the new beginning.
I am a co-creator with God, and it is a new
*   heaven that comes,*
as the Good Will of God is expressed on earth
*   through me.*
It is the kingdom of light, love, peace, and
*   understanding.*
And I am doing my part to reveal its reality.

I begin with me.
I am a living soul and the presence of God dwells
*   in me, as me.*
I am one with God and the fullness of the
*   kingdom is mine.*
In truth I am the supreme expression of God.

What is true of me is true of everyone,
for God is all and all is God.
I see only the Spirit of God in every soul.
And to every man, woman, and child on earth I say:
I love you, for you are me. You are my Holy Self.

I now open my heart,
and let the pure essence of unconditional love
*   pour out.*
I see it as a Golden Light radiating from the
*   center of my being,*
and I feel its divine vibration in and through me,
*   above and below me.*

I am one with the light.
I am filled with the light.
I am illumined by the light.
I am the light of the world.

With purpose of mind, I send forth the light.
I let the radiance go before me to join the other
*   lights.*
I know this is happening all over the world at this
*   moment.*
I see the merging lights.
There is now one light. We are the light of the world.

The one light of love, peace, and understanding is
*   moving.*
It flows across the face of the earth,
touching and illuminating everyone in the
*   shadow of the illusion.*
And where there was darkness, there is now the
*   light of Reality.*

And the radiance grows, permeating, saturating
*   every form of life.*
There is only the vibration of one perfect life now.
All the kingdoms of the earth respond,
And the planet is alive with light and love.

There is total oneness,
And in this oneness we speak the word.

Let the sense of separation be dissolved.
Let humankind be returned to Godkind.

Let peace come forth in every mind.
Let love flow forth from every heart.
Let forgiveness reign in every soul.
Let understanding be the common bond.

And now from the light of the world,
the one Presence and Power of the universe
*   responds.*
The activity of God is healing and harmonizing
*   Planet Earth.*
Omnipotence is made manifest.

I am seeing the salvation of the planet before my
*   very eyes,*
as all false beliefs and error patterns are dissolved.
The sense of separation is no more; the healing
*   has taken place,*
and the world is returned to sanity.

This is the beginning of Peace on Earth and Good
*   Will toward all,*
As love flows forth from every heart.
forgiveness reigns in every soul,
and all hearts and minds are one in perfect
*   understanding.*

It is done. And it is so.

———

Yes, love does flow, forgiveness does reign, and our hearts and minds are forever one in perfect understanding. And that very bright light on the horizon is our future. Where is this horizon in time and space? It is that point where the heaven and earth meet, the joining together of perfect energy and perfect form, and it is now—not to come but *now*. That's the great secret that we have now discovered.

In our journey we have crossed that point, that distant horizon. We don't have to be concerned about what is waiting for us around the corner, or a few years down the road because *we are now in the light*. And as we continue in the light we realize that *our future is now*. We rest in the *now*—the only time there is—and we see that we shall indeed live in a perfect world, for it is eternally unfolding from where we are at this very instant.

18

REMINDERS

G od is. All there is is God, and God is good,
loving, and forever expressing perfection
through me.

I am God being me. I am an immortal spiritual being
eternally one with my Source.

The meaning and purpose of life is happiness and joy.
I am happy. I am joyful. My life is wonderful!

There is no death, only a continuation of eternal life.

I am the master, time is the servant.

This is a loving universe where every good and perfect possibility exists.

Nothing is impossible. I can do, be, and have all things good, true, and beautiful.

I have never done anything wrong. I forgive myself for thinking so.

I lift my consciousness into the higher frequencies each day by contemplating my glorious Holy Self.

My mind and heart are in tune with the Angel of the Presence.

I do everything for the incredible joy and fun of it.

There's no sense worrying about anything, everything's just fine. I believe this with all my heart.

I do not identify myself as a physical body. I am pure spirit, pure energy, and I concentrate on the truth of my being. I dwell only on the Cause within.

God is perfect life. There is only one life. My life is God's life. Therefore, my life is perfect.

The energy of inspiration is flowing through me now. I am inspired!

My vision is fixed only on the greatest and grandest in life.

I speak only uplifting words and use my power for the greater good of all.

I love myself and everyone else unconditionally.

I forgive everyone without exception. Resentment is no longer a part of my life.

I approve of myself and all others as spiritual beings temporarily clothed in physical form.

There is nothing to fear in my life—today, tomorrow, or forever. I am safe in God.

I am the Light unto my world, both inner and outer. Wherever I am at this moment is only Light, and darkness cannot enter.

I will, I see, I create, I love—purposely, clearly, beautifully, and unconditionally.

I live in love, with love, as love. Love is all there is.

I live with wisdom. I am the wisdom of my Self in action. I am wise.

I am consciously aware that whatever it is I seek is already a part of the reality of my Self. It is done!

I MUST have unlimited health, wealth, and happiness for it is a CERTAINTY of who and what I AM—and I see the MUST principle at work in everyone else.

I recognize my true worth and do not wish to be someone other than who I am, for God is not complete without me.

I am guiltless and blameless. I am deserving because I know who I am.

In my true humility I am open and receptive to new ideas.

I revere my livingness. I cherish the opportunity to reawaken to all the joys that life has to offer.

I have everything now because I have been given the Kingdom of Energies, and I give up the belief that there is anything missing in my life.

I trust the Master Self within to take care of everything in my life.

I leave all decisions to the One within who knows.

I accept all that I AM and all that I HAVE. I accept my completeness.

The bridge between the inner and outer is complete and the activity of God is the only power at work in my life.

I dedicate my life to the Spirit of God within, my Holy Self, and keep my mind focused on this loving Presence that I AM.

To reach the human scene Spirit must move through individual consciousness. The transforming power of God is radiating through me now.

I have done my part to complete the revolution from darkness to light. I am a co-creator with God.

APPENDIX

CHART OF
THE ANGELS

1. **Angel of Unconditional Love and Freedom.** *Purpose:* teaches harmlessness and functions as the fountain for the outpouring of Universal Love; serves as the master of the other Causal Powers; assists in the realization of your True Self and the recognition of that Self in others.

2. **Angel of Illusion and Reality.** *Purpose:* helps you to separate false from true in your life through the energy of creative intelligence; the illuminating principle which releases the mind from bondage and enables one to be aware of the divine plan.

3. **Angel of Creative Wisdom.** *Purpose:* the ability to solve problems quickly; imparts spiritual wisdom to

your consciousness by providing the bridge between the higher and lower natures; ensures that judgment is clear and correct; stimulates instinctive action.

4. **Angel of Abundance.** *Purpose:* the distributor of divine substance embodying all supply, Love, beauty, and Power in constant radiation.

5. **Angel of Power and Authority.** *Purpose:* great energy and determination, strong decisiveness with reliance on the Will of God in every situation.

6. **Angel of Spiritual Understanding.** *Purpose:* lifts vibration of consciousness to level of spiritual perception. It is the energy of openmindedness, enabling the aspirant to learn deep esoteric truths and become a teacher of knowledge.

7. **Angel of Loving Relationships.** *Purpose:* ensures that you make the correct choice in relationships; the primary energy in courtship and marriage.

8. **Angel of Victory and Triumph.** *Purpose:* the energy of achievement and the archetype of the conqueror; helps you to meet your objective with determination; stimulates tenacity and resolution.

9. **Angel of Order and Harmony.** *Purpose:* the peace vibration in consciousness; helps you to maintain balance and fairness in all situations; inspires you to live with integrity.

10. **Angel of Discernment.** *Purpose:* this angel works best in moments of solitude to train your mind to be prudent and judicious and to help you to take actions based on proper discernment.

11. **Angel of Cycles and Solutions.** *Purpose:* the ability to accept change and move into expansive cycles with the attitude that nothing but absolute good is taking place; also called the Energy of Miracles.

12. **Angel of Spiritual Strength and Will.** *Purpose:* helps you to have the mental will, emotional determination, and physical fortitude to follow the spiritual path regardless of worldly temptations.

13. **Angel of Renunciation and Regeneration.** *Purpose:* provides the energy of surrender, showing you the ease and beauty of "having nothing in order to possess everything."

14. **Angel of Death and Rebirth.** *Purpose:* called the energy of metamorphosis, this angel helps you to cross out the ego and realize your identity as a spiritual being.

15. **Angel of Patience and Acceptance.** *Purpose:* provides the energy that enables you to trust the divine process with total acceptance of "come what may," living day to day with calm equanimity.

16. **Angel of Materiality and Temptation.** *Purpose:* helps you to "stay gounded" until you are spiritually ready to awaken into fourth-dimensional consciousness while protecting you from going too far with a preoccupation with effects.

17. **Angel of Courage and Perseverance.** *Purpose:* provides the energy of steadfastness—the courage to live only the Truth of Being and to persevere in that consciousness regardless of what is going on around you.

18. **Angel of Service and Synthesis.** *Purpose:* to motivate you to greater service to the world and help you to understand why service is a primary requisite for receiving the Energy of the Master Self.

19. **Angel of Imagination and Liberation.** *Purpose:* teaches you to image abstractly and see with the inner eye; strengthens the spiritual vision enabling you to see the Truth of the finished Kingdom—a higher vision of Reality that can be fully manifest on the third-dimensional plane.

20. **Angel of Truth and Enlightenment.** *Purpose:* seeks to unite the lower and higher natures; the energy of the transcendental consciousness, where individuality replaces personality; the healing energy to maintain wholeness of body.

21. **Angel of the Creative Word.** *Purpose:* releases energy to move consciousness above miscreations into the realm of Cause, where the spoken word can be used to correct situations and settle matters for the good of all.

22. **Angel of Success.** *Purpose:* provides the energy to be truly successful in your field of "true place"—the energy of dominion through self-knowledge.

NOTES

INTRODUCTION

1. Newton Dillaway, ed., *The Gospel of Emerson* (Wakefield, Mass.: Montrose Press, 1949), 8.

2. Ibid., 37.

ONE: POINT OF DEPARTURE

1. Elaine Pagels, *The Gnostic Gospels* (New York: Vintage Books, 1981), 40.

2. Ibid., 41.

3. Manly P. Hall, *The Secret Teachings of All Ages: An Encyclopedic Outline of Masonic, Hermetic, Quabbalistic, and Rosicrucian Symbolical Philosophy*

(Los Angeles: The Philosophical Research Society, Inc., 1977), CLXXIX.

4. Pagels, 161.

5. Alice A. Bailey, *Esoteric Healing* (New York: Lucis Publishing Company, 1953), 567.

6. Jan Price, *The Other Side of Death* (New York: Fawcett Columbine/Ballantine, 1996), 84.

7. *The Quartus Report*, vol. xv, September–October 1996 (Boerne, Tex.: The Quartus Foundation), 7.

TWO: THE ROOTS OF GOOD AND EVIL

1. John Jocelyn, *Meditations on the Signs of the Zodiac* (San Francisco: Harper & Row, Publishers, 1970), 171–172.

2. Ibid., 172.

3. Alice A. Bailey, *Esoteric Psychology,* vol. II (New York: Lucis Publishing Company, 1960), 576.

4. Alice A. Bailey, *A Treatise on Cosmic Fire* (New York: Lucis Publishing Company, 1964), 947.

5. Manly P. Hall, *The Secret Teachings of All Ages: An Encyclopedic Outline of Masonic, Hermetic, Quabbalistic, and Rosicrucian Symbolical Philosophy* (Los Angeles: Philosophical Research Society, 1977), CCIV.

THREE: THE NEW TRANSCENDENTALISTS

1. Joseph L. Blau, *Men and Movements in*

American Philosophy (New York: Prentice-Hall, Inc., 1952), 111.

2. Lewis Mumford, Selected and with an Introduction by, *Ralph Waldo Emerson: Essays and Journals* (Garden City, N.Y.: International Collectors Library, 1968), 25.

3. Newton Dillaway, ed., *The Gospel of Emerson* (Wakefield, Mass.: The Montrose Press, 1949), 13–14.

4. Irwin Edman, Introduction, *Essays by Ralph Waldo Emerson* (New York: Harper & Row, Publishers, 1951, originally published by Thomas Y. Crowell Company, Inc., 1926), 33.

5. Ibid., 51.

6. Ibid., 56.

7. Dillaway, 71.

8. Ibid., 71.

9. Edman, 74.

10. Dillaway, 61.

11. Ibid., 62.

12. Ibid., 63.

13. Louis Pauwels and Jacques Bergier, *The Morning of the Magicians* (New York: A Scarborough Book, Stein and Day, Publishers, 1983), 296.

FOUR: BEGINNING THE JOURNEY WITH JOY

1. John Randolph Price, *The Angels Within Us* (New York: Fawcett Columbine/Ballantine, 1993), 210.

2. A. C. Bhaktivedanta Swami Prabhupada,

trans., *Bhagavad-Gita as It Is* (New York: Bhak-tivedanta Book Trust, 1968), 226.

3. William Gorman, ed., *The Great Ideas, A Synopticon of Great Books of the Western World*, vol. 1 (Chicago: Encyclopedia Britannica, 1952), 687.

4. Newton Dillaway, ed., *The Gospel of Emerson* (Wakefield, Mass.: Montrose Press, 1949), 10.

5. Ibid., 30.

6. Alice A. Bailey, *Discipleship in the New Age,* vol. I (New York: Lucis Publishing Company, 1972), 170.

7. Ibid., 176.

8. Ibid., 565.

9. Jan Price, *The Other Side of Death* (New York: Fawcett Columbine/Ballantine, 1996), 64.

10. Michael Ryan, "Who Is Great?" in *Parade* magazine, Walter Anderson, ed. (New York: Parade Publications, June 16, 1996), 4.

11. John Randolph Price, *The Superbeings* (mass-market edition, New York: Fawcett Crest, Ballantine Books, 1988; trade edition: Carlsbad, Cal.: Hay House, Inc., 1997), xxiii.

FIVE: MOVING FROM FORM TO ENERGY

1. Nick Herbert, *Quantum Reality* (New York: Anchor Books, Doubleday, 1987), 18.

2. Ibid., 166.

3. Ibid., 167.

4. Ibid., 189.

5. Ibid., 192.

6. Alice A. Bailey, *Esoteric Healing* (New York: Lucis Publishing Company, 1953), 579.

7. Ibid., 613.

8. Alice A. Bailey, *Discipleship in the New Age,* vol. I, (New York: Lucis Publishing Company, 1972), 433.

9. *A Course in Miracles,* vol. 2, *Workbook for Students* (Tiburon, Cal.: Foundation for Inner Peace, 1975), 372.

EIGHT: THE MENTAL REALM

1. Dr. Douglas Baker, *The Theory and Practice of Meditation* (Herts, Eng.: Douglas Baker, 1975), 133.

2. John Randolph Price, *The Angels Within Us* (New York: Fawcett Columbine/Ballantine, 1993), 37.

3. Alice A. Bailey, *A Treatise on Cosmic Fire* (New York: Lucis Publishing Company, 1964), 310.

4. Manly P. Hall, *The Phoenix* (Los Angeles: Hall, 1931), 49.

5. Ibid., 50.

6. Orest Bedrij, *You* (Warwick, N.Y.: Amity House, 1988), 34.

NINE: LIVING WITH LOVE

1. William Gorman, ed., *The Great Ideas, A Synopticon of Great Books of the Western World,* vol. 2 (Chicago: Encyclopedia Britannica, 1952), 1057.

2. Ibid., 1058.

3. Prof. Charles F. Horne, Ph.D., With an Historical Survey and Descriptions by, *The Sacred Books and Early Literature of the East, Volume II, Egypt* (New York: Parke, Austin, and Lipscomb, Inc., 1917), 69.

4. John Randolph Price, *The Workbook for Self-Mastery*, formerly titled *The Planetary Commission* (Carlsbad, Cal.: Hay House, Inc., 1997), 136.

5. Alice A. Bailey, *The Externalization of the Hierarchy* (New York: Lucis Publishing Company, 1958), 335.

6. *The Quartus Report,* vol. xiv, no. 11 (Boerne, Tex.: The Quartus Foundation, November–December 1995), 8.

7. Eric Butterworth, *Life Is for Loving* (New York: Harper & Row, Publishers, 1973), 91–92.

TEN: LIVING WITH FORGIVENESS

1. A. C. Bhaktivedanta Swami Prabhupada, trans., *Bhagavad-Gita as It Is* (New York: Bhaktivedanta Book Trust, 1968), 235.

2. *A Course in Miracles,* vol. II, *Workbook for Students* (Tiburon, Cal.: Foundation for Inner Peace, 1975), 355.

3. Ibid., 357.

4. John Randolph Price, *The Angels Within Us* (New York: Fawcett Columbine/Ballantine, 1993), 14–15.

5. John Randolph Price, *Angel Energy* (New York: Fawcett Columbine/Ballantine, 1995), 55.

ELEVEN: LIVING WITH WISDOM

1. Lionel Giles, Litt.D., trans., *The Analects of Confucius* (Shanghai, China: Printed for the members of the Limited Editions Club by the Commercial Press, 1933), 2.

2. Ibid., 13.

3. Jan Price, *The Other Side of Death* (New York: Fawcett Columbine/Ballantine, 1996), 33.

4. John Randolph Price, *Practical Spirituality* (Carlsbad, Cal.: Hay House, Inc., 1996), 91.

5. Ibid., 56.

6. *A Course in Miracles, vol. II, Workbook for Students* (Tiburon, Cal.: Foundation for Inner Peace, 1975), 179.

TWELVE: PAY FOR IT AND TAKE WHAT YOU WANT

1. Newton Dillaway, ed., *The Gospel of Emerson* (Wakefield, Mass.: Montrose Press, 1949), 46.

2. John Randolph Price, *Angel Energy* (New York: Fawcett Columbine/Ballantine, 1995), 5.

3. Ibid., 13.

4. Ibid., 106.

5. Jan Price, *The Other Side of Death* (New York: Fawcett Columbine/Ballantine, 1996), 19.

FOURTEEN: THE MEANING OF WORTHINESS

1. Jan Price, *The Other Side of Death* (New York: Fawcett Columbine/Ballantine, 1996), 76.

FIFTEEN: ONE GOD IS ENOUGH

1. *A Course in Miracles,* vol. I, Text (Tiburon, Cal.: Foundation for Inner Peace, 1975), 32.

SIXTEEN: LIVING THE GOOD LIFE

1. John Randolph Price, *A Spiritual Philosophy for the New World* (Carlsbad, Cal.: Hay House, Inc., 1997), 18.

ABOUT THE AUTHOR

JOHN RANDOLPH PRICE is an internationally known visionary, lecturer, and bestselling author of more than a dozen books published in many languages. With clarity and penetrating insight he probes the philosophic mysteries of Ageless Wisdom, and shows us how to apply the ancient and eternal truths to living positively, fully, and joyfully in today's world.

In 1981 he and his wife Jan formed The Quartus Foundation, a spiritual research and communications organization based in the Texas hill country near San Antonio. They are also the originators of "World Healing Day"—a global mind-link for peace that began at noon Greenwich time on December 31, 1986, and has continued to be a yearly event in over a hundred countries.

For information about workshops conducted by John and Jan Price and their bi-monthly publication The Quartus Report, *please contact The Quartus Foundation, P.O. Box 1768, Boerne, Texas 78006.*